Table of Contents

About Denny

Sometimes God gives a man an astoundingly powerful message. God blessed Denny Kenaston with such a message. He preached it often and when he did men and women fell before God in thanksgiving and with a yearning to be what God desired. It was a God thing. Then in 2012 Denny unexpectedly died of brain cancer.

Millions of women needed this gloriously encouraging message. Jackie (Denny's beloved wife) and Debi Pearl, the internationally bestselling author of the Help Meet Book series worked together to put it in print.

God went hunting for Denny back in 1972 when he was in a grip of an immoral hippie lifestyle filled with drugs and alcohol. Denny and Jackie were gloriously transformed by the power of the gospel which led them to marry and head off to Bible College within months of coming to know the Savior. During their 40-plus years together, the Lord blessed them with eight children, and many grandchildren. Denny was extremely passionate about the home, missions, and revival. Over one million of Denny's messages have been sent out across the world in cassette or CD format. Now, combined with online downloads and the fact that other ministries have been given

5

permission to distribute them, it is impossible to estimate the number of people impacted through his ministry.

For over 40 years, Jackie was Denny's Hidden Woman, always busy at home rearing the family, feeding guests, welcoming those who were in need, and praying for the man God called to this work.

As a widow, Jackie stays busy doing hospice work, speaking at women's meetings, helping to organize retreats, and traveling. Her commitment to teaching others how to have a beautiful marriage has only grown stronger since Denny's death. Her prayer is that this book will influence your life positively for his kingdom!

When Jackie read the draft of this book she said, "It was wonderful and totally seamless. I could not tell what was his and what was yours."

Before You Read...

All passages in this font were written by Debi Pearl.

All passages in this font were transcribed from Denny's audio "The Hidden Woman."

*If ever there were a time
when a man needed a dear
wife to stand beside him and
say, "I'm here. I'm with you.
I'm behind you. I'll help you"*
that time is now...

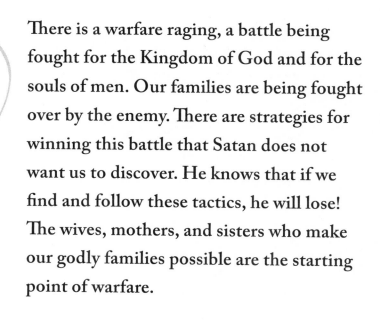

Chapter One

Battle for the Kingdom

Proverbs 31:10 Who can find a virtuous woman?
for her price is far above rubies.

There is a warfare raging, a battle being fought for the Kingdom of God and for the souls of men. Our families are being fought over by the enemy. There are strategies for winning this battle that Satan does not want us to discover. He knows that if we find and follow these tactics, he will lose! The wives, mothers, and sisters who make our godly families possible are the starting point of warfare.

*M*y desire is to open your eyes, inspire you, and compel you with the truth of God's Word, to help you understand and believe that you are not "just a woman." You are a very important part of God's plan. In many ways, your role could be more powerful than a man's, and in many cases you could reap more reward. We do not understand God's economy; we have only glimpses of how he works, so it is very important that we do what he says.

The powerful woman mentioned in Proverbs 31 demonstrates the home-front strategies. There is no doubt about it: a godly woman's effect on the outcome of the war against the family is staggering. Satan knows this, and he also knows woman's weakness. In order to fight the good fight, it is clearly important to know how Satan will come at you.

What is woman's weakness? *God gave us an example that clearly spells out how women can be deceived and how devastating it is when they give in to their weakness.* Satan knows very well how to deceive each woman just like he knew how to deceive Eve in the Garden. Satan continues to come to every Eve with that same questioning and seducing spirit, saying, "Yea, hath God not said?" *It was Eve who handed the reins of God's kingdom over to Satan by simply wanting to be wiser and go deeper into "more spiritual" things. The issue is always the same: If it doesn't seem spiritual or good, a woman wonders if it is right. She questions God. Women, just like Eve, find it hard to believe that God really means what he says if it doesn't suit them. Women need the direct command clarified; they stumble if it doesn't seem fair or appears unjust. Besides this weakness of the "fairness sentiment," teachers and preachers like to tickle the ears of women with spiritual tenderness and do so by twisting Greek and Hebrew and/or by teaching that changing culture makes God's words outdated, therefore of no consequence. After all, how could God expect a woman to submit to her husband? Serve her husband? Or think that she was simply created to be his helper? Why shouldn't the man be HER helper if she is smarter and more capable? It sounds primitive to think of a woman in this role. When the biblical role of man and woman is brought up in court during a divorce, it becomes a laughing matter. Evil wins. But God will hold court someday, and I want to be found on HIS side.*

Like Eve of old, women today are convinced to take a bite out of the new fruit, not realizing it is the same old fruit and the same old curse. The fruit looked pleasant to Eve's eyes. She was promised an exalted position of wisdom she had never known . She took the bait. Life was forever changed by Eve's decision. Oh, the confusion that has come from the choices women have made in leaving the supportive role of wife and mother. *My goal is not to lay the burden on women, rather it is to focus on the facts of God's Word. GOD*

> *God will hold court someday, and I want to be found on HIS side.*

wrote the marriage plan—how it works best and why we must adhere to his plan. He did it for ALL our good, not just the husband's well-being. It is good for the wife, and it is very good for the children. God's marriage plan works. He laid out the plan before Eve was even created. In fact, God designed and then created woman in such a way as to fulfill this role. God wrote in Genesis 2:

> And the LORD God said, It is not good that the man should be alone; I will make him an help meet for him.
>
> And the LORD God caused a deep sleep to fall upon Adam, and he slept: and he took one of his ribs, and closed up the flesh instead thereof; And the rib, which the LORD God had taken from man, made he a woman, and brought her unto the man. And Adam said, This is now bone of my bones, and flesh of my flesh: she shall be called Woman, because she was taken out of Man.

I would never have dared to write these next verses. God says things that many do not like, and 1 Corinthians 11:7-10 is such a passage:

> For a man indeed ought not to cover his head, forasmuch as he is the image and glory of God: but the woman is the glory of the man. For the man is not of the woman; but the woman of the man. Neither was the man created for the woman; but the woman for the man. For this cause ought the woman to have power on her head because of the angels.

Did you notice the phrase "because of the angels"?

I have no idea what this means, but I do know that one of the reasons God established the role of a wife under the man's leadership is "because of the angels." Long before there were man and woman, there were male angels, good and bad. The Bible gives us several accounts of giants, men of renown, seducing strange flesh and so on. We know that there was a great war between God and a a number of angels that chose to rebel. People seem to think God just started "having a life" when man was created, but man is just one thing in God's forever history. There was eternity past long before life as we know it came to be. Very little of eternity past is recorded in the Bible, but God does warn us over and over that there is still fallout from these fallen creatures and we are to be ready to resist them. Satan is the kingpin of this gang of outlaw angels, and he is after your marriage, your soul, and—an even greater victory—your children's souls. The passage "because of the angels" just hints that there is some kind of spiritual warfare that we don't know anything about concerning a woman remaining under her husband's protective spiritual authority.

Did you notice the phrase "because of the angels"?

God's Word says in Ephesians 6:12:

> **For we wrestle not against flesh and blood, but against principalities, against powers, against the rulers of the darkness of this world, against spiritual wickedness in high places.**

Our own feelings, our husband, or even our situation is not our real problem; the real issue is evil spirits that war against us, wooing us to question God. So God set in place a hierarchy of leadership that is a protection for the wife and that brings extreme satisfaction and joy to the entire family.

God's plan has nothing to do with who deserves to be first or who is the smartest or most capable. The thing we are missing today is the fact that it is GOD's plan, it is GOD's will, and it will work if we do it God's way. God always has a reason. It is not ours to question God. It seems everyone has an exception clause. Every family, every wife, and every situation wants to change the plan, but it remains written in the book—God's book—which is the very WORDS of God.

Divorce is at an all-time high, which results in children growing up sitting in a house alone, watching trash on TV while eating trash because Mama is not there to oversee her charges. God says in Proverbs 29:15:

... but a child left to himself bringeth his mother to shame.

The result of a woman being out from under her husband's headship is children who are insecure, emotionally tense, full of anger, unproductive, and unable to have wholesome relationships. Mothers are the caretakers of these little souls, and when Mom is out of the home there will be consequences that are unhealable. The devastating results are becoming the norm as more children are growing up and reaching adulthood emotionally ill. Eternity will reveal the full extent of the damage done, all because people have left God's original plan for the home and thus opened up the family to the wiles of the devil.

Being a help meet—a real help meet—gives a woman an amazing amount of influence. She can and will make a big, positive difference. Being a good help meet is an eternal position that will reap eternal benefits.

If God wanted us to see the spirit world and the battle that rages, he would have made that possible; but he wants us to learn to trust him, the opposite of what Eve did when she questioned that God knew what was best for her. Although it is not given to us to understand it all, it is required that we obey God. I was thinking recently about all the instruction given to husbands and fathers. I know that many of the men may feel overwhelmed with what God requires of them. If ever there was a time when a man needed a dear wife to stand beside him and say, *"I'm here. I'm with you. I'm behind you. I'll help you,"* that time is now. *I bid you now,* come, be a Hidden Woman. Come, be a Virtuous Woman. Come, be a powerful, supportive wife. Come out of the shadows and stand beside your man. He needs your help like never before.

Put your hand in his hand and say, "I'm with you."

From the time I was Six or Seven years old, if any one spoke to me concerning marrying, I used to say, I thought I never should, "Because I should never find such a Woman as my Father had."
—An excerpt from John Wesley's journal

Chapter Two

God's Purpose for
Women

Proverbs 31:11,12 The heart of her husband doth safely trust in her, so that he shall have no need of spoil. She will do him good and not evil all the days of her life.

The role of a godly woman is a paradox. It doesn't make sense; that is the way paradoxes are. The role of a godly woman is to be supportive. That means it is often hidden and unknown to others. Yet her power and her influence often exceed that of a man whose role is public.

The child that never learns to obey his parents in the home will not obey God or man out of the home.
—Susanna Wesley

Remember Susanna Wesley, *the mother of John and Charles Wesley, two of the most famous men of God of their time. They are fathers of the Methodist movement. Both men gave their mother credit for having raised them to love and honor God. Susanna Wesley's influence changed millions of people's lives, yet she was simply a wife and mother, a hidden woman.*

Consider now the path to greatness that Jesus taught. He said greatness comes as we live the life of a servant, giving of ourselves. Jesus gave the example of washing someone's feet, and said "this is greatness."

John 13:13–17 Ye call me Master and Lord: and ye say well; for so I am. If I then, your Lord and Master, have washed your feet; ye also ought to wash one another's feet. For I have given you an example, that ye should do as I have done to you. Verily, verily, I say unto you, The servant is not greater than his lord; neither he that is sent greater than he that sent him. If ye know these things, happy are ye if ye do them.

Did you ever consider the life of a good angel? An angel is hidden most of the time, never seen by us. Most of the time people don't even know when an angel has done something to minister to them. God gets all the glory from these heavenly beings. They are concealed from human view, yet God sees their work, and they do a myriad of tasks for him.

Imagine an accident that is about to happen and angels are there on the scene, yet we cannot see them. They grab the steering wheel and guide the car to safety. When the car stops, we know we have been spared, and we bow our heads and thank God for caring for us. Not a word is said to the angel, yet it was his obedience to God, his act on our behalf, that saved us.

Ah, if we could let God purify our motives and give us eternal eyes that serve the Lord, as do the angels. Someday it will all become clear.

What about the life of Joshua? For 42 years he served Moses faithfully. Very little is mentioned about Joshua until Moses died. Do you think Moses could have served God the way he did if he had not had Joshua to serve and support him? No, Moses needed Joshua. For years he was known only as "Joshua, the servant of Moses," until later, when God appointed him to lead the people of Israel after Moses' death.

> **Exodus 33:11 And the LORD spake unto Moses face to face, as a man speaketh unto his friend. And he turned again into the camp: but his servant Joshua, the son of Nun, a young man, departed not out of the tabernacle.**

God's ordained purpose for the woman is to be _for the man._

Every military man knows that if you don't have a solid support unit working behind the scenes you will not be able to win the war. This is yet another example of the vital role of a woman. In fact, in a battle, if a soldier doesn't have a support unit in place, he won't even go out on the battlefield. He can't go out. He isn't prepared. He would be a fool to try alone.

For every soldier, there must be food, water, medical supplies, plus everything to keep the company and equipment moving such as gas and oil. Then he has to have the tools to fight the war or there would be no reason to go forth. It takes more men and more careful planning to provide behind the front lines support than it does the ones actually in the battle.

God's ordained purpose for the woman is to be that behind the scenes support for her man. _This purpose is clearly revealed in Genesis 2 when God explains that it is not good for the man to be alone. He said in effect, "I will make him a helper perfectly suited for him. She will be exactly what he needs. She will come alongside him and help him." Know for certain, woman (wife) was created to be the support; her divine calling is to be a helper to her man._

Put yourself in Eve's place for just a moment when she was created: she was not, and then she was. All of a sudden she came into existence. I imagine when she opened up her eyes she must have looked into the face of God who made her. There was probably a question in her mind: "What is this? Who am I? What am I here for?"

I think God probably instructed her before he took her to the man. The Bible says God made her, and then took her to the man.

God might have said "Eve, I am God. I made you. I took you out of that man over there, who is sleeping. I made you because he needs you. I made you for him, Eve. Do you understand? You will be his helper."

His Heart Safely Trusts in Her

Proverbs 31:10–12 Who can find a virtuous woman? for her price is far above rubies. The heart of her husband doth safely trust in her, so that he shall have no need of spoil. She will do him good and not evil all the days of her life.

Here we see a picture of a beautiful woman whose life is all wrapped up in being a help meet for her husband. *"His heart doth safely trust in her."* He doesn't have a worry or fret about his wife. He knows she will never leave him. Her commitment to him is sure. She will spend their money carefully. She will never do anything that would bring him dishonor. She will be a good mother of his children. He has confidence in her, knowing she will be his loving, supportive wife all the days of her life, just as the Scripture describes.

Her heart's desire is to live for her husband and please him. She would do him good and not evil. When everyone else questions him, she stands firm. He will feel confident in her commitment to him; he will be open to hearing her opinion because he knows that in the end she will stand with him. How long will she be his most trusted friend? "Until death do us part." He can count on her and trust her with his heart. He knows what her responses will be in the thick and thin of life. *He knows when he is away she will guide the home according to <u>his heart</u>. She does not manipulate her husband with mild deception to do things to suit her will. He feels her honor and knows her honor will bring him honor from others.* This is a very valuable woman described in this proverb, a priceless jewel and a crown on her husband's head.

Regardless of what a man must face, he can do so with confidence when he has a woman who stands with him.

Proverbs 12:4 A virtuous woman is a crown to her husband: but she that maketh ashamed is as rottenness in his bones.

The God-ordained role of a woman is the foundation stone that must be laid if you are going to have a peaceful, godly home. It is God's revealed purpose for woman, plain and simple. The only way you will ever see your children grow to love and honor God with wisdom and confidence is by hiding yourself in this beautiful purpose for which you were made. This is what being a hidden woman is.

There is a strong source of strength that charges the mental and emotional batteries of a man when he has a woman like this. I assure you—I guarantee you—this is truth. *Regardless of what a man must face, he can do so with confidence when he has a woman who stands with him. He doesn't second-guess himself, hesitate with uncertainty, or just refuse to do a project due to fear of failure if he has a woman there telling him he can do it and that she will help.*

I think you all know that these statements stand on the assumption that the husband is not bodily harming his wife or failing to act as a natural sexual partner for her, or (if capable) neglecting to provide necessary provision for her and the children to survive.

Exodus 21:10–11 ...her food, her raiment, and her duty of marriage, shall he not diminish. And if he do not these three unto her, then shall she go out free without money.

1 Corinthians 7:4 The wife hath not power of her own body, but the husband: and likewise also the husband hath not power of his own body, but the wife. Defraud ye not one the other, except it be with consent for a time, that ye may give yourselves to fasting and prayer; and come together again, that Satan tempt you not for your incontinency.

1 Timothy 5:8 But if any provide not for his own, and specially for those of his own house, he hath denied the faith, and is worse than an infidel.

The heart of her husband
doth safely trust in her.

Chapter Three

Your Hand in
His Hand

**Behind every great man
is an extraordinary, hidden help meet**

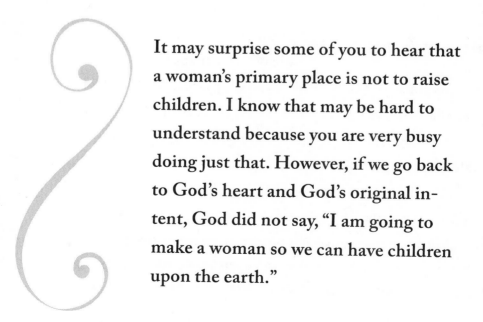

It may surprise some of you to hear that a woman's primary place is not to raise children. I know that may be hard to understand because you are very busy doing just that. However, if we go back to God's heart and God's original intent, God did not say, "I am going to make a woman so we can have children upon the earth."

God said,

Your primary purpose is for your husband. Although you may be busy raising children, I want to encourage you, do not lose sight of your husband. He is the reason you are here. Remember that both you and the children are in your husband's care. God has given you to him. A man would not ignore his boss in order to take care of the other employees. If necessary, he would ignore the other employees under his authority in order to hear what his boss is saying and get new directions.

> *Do not lose sight of your husband. He is the reason you are here.*

Many wives lose their focus as time goes on. Because of the busy demands of motherhood, or because of a strained relationship with your husband, or perhaps by listening to seducing spirits, you can be led away. Maybe you have reached a place where you've said to yourself, "Okay, I can't figure this guy out. I can't get along with him. So I'm going to forget him and focus on raising my children."

I can tell you, it won't work out like you hope it will. You are here for your husband. You can't just throw off your God-ordained purpose and choose another. *There is an unseen war involving principalities, powers, and rulers of darkness. It takes a mama and a daddy to protect the family.*

Imagine just for a moment that you are on your deathbed.

You can't just throw off your God-ordained purpose and choose another.

You are dying, and you know it. It's all over. You've said goodbye to your children and your husband. This is it; you're gone. As you enter Heaven's glories, God stops you and says, "Wait a minute, my child. Your work on earth is not finished. You need to go back. Your husband needs you. He needs your love and support, and he needs you to stand beside him. You must go back and serve your husband. It's not time for you to come into Heaven yet."

All of a sudden you wake up again and you are back in your body, alive once more. You hear the faint voice of your husband beside the bed crying. He is saying, "Oh, God! Please God, give me back my wife. I need my wife. I don't know if I'm going to make it without her."

You hear the voice of your husband saying those words and you remember the voice of God telling you to go back and serve your husband. What will you do now? What will you do?

You will rise up. You will love and serve your husband all the days of your life like you never did before. Why? Because God spoke to you face to face and gave you the commission all over again to love and serve your husband. He said, "This is what I want you to do."

Remember the story of doubting Thomas? Isn't

it ironic that although Thomas was a good, faithful man he is remembered as being the doubting disciple? When the disciples told Thomas of seeing Jesus alive, Thomas told them he just couldn't believe it was true. Thomas said, "Unless I put my own hands into the prints of the nails, I will not believe." Then eight days later Jesus appeared again and this time Thomas was there. Jesus offered his hands to Thomas and said, "Now do you believe?" Then Jesus gently rebuked Thomas for his unbelief.

John 20:29 Jesus saith unto him, Thomas, because thou hast seen me, thou hast believed: blessed are they that have not seen, and yet have believed.

Oh, that we could simply believe God when he gave us his written instruction, as if he came down in his divine appearance and told us his will for our lives. If we could only embrace with the same devotion his written Word when he tells us his will for our lives without being like Thomas.

Hebrews 11 is a chapter listing those Old Testament saints who walked by faith. God called their believing him RIGHTEOUSNESS.

There is an American proverb which is often quoted in the context of history. It goes like this:

Behind every great man is a great woman.

This is a true statement. Perhaps it needs to be sanctified a bit, but it is a true statement.

Woman is a powerful creature. I doubt you realize just how powerful you really are, for good and for bad. I believe that Satan has been lying to you, making you think you don't matter that much.

In a secular sense, the above proverb often refers to a strong woman who is motivating and pushing her husband to achieve. You can find that

> *Jezebel... was committed to her husband, but for her own good.*

story many times in history: a man who gained power because of a woman who was pushing him to succeed, so she could rise to the top as well. *We have a memorable example of such a woman found in God's Word. Her name was Jezebel. Yes, you know of her, as do most people who have ever opened a Bible. She was committed to her husband, but for her own ends.*

The Great Manipulator

Jezebel is a byword for a woman who is altogether godless. The Bible describes the upbringing of Jezebel as being careless. Careless—her mama was careless in leaving her daughter to herself, she was careless in what she let her daughter do, and she was careless in what she let her wear and how she let her talk. Her mama did not carefully oversee her daughter, and

the results were that Jezebel's very name is the description of an evil woman. Oh, the power a mama has in raising her children!

Jezebel grew up and married a king. Now she had power to do as she wished. What people don't realize about Jezebel is that many things she did were for her gods. She was very dedicated to her religion. She also worked hard to bring about success for her husband. She even manipulated circumstances so that when he was depressed and unhappy about not getting something that he wanted, she made it happen. One of the stories told concerning Jezebel is how she used the system and her husband's authority to take another man's land to give to her husband. It was a mean, selfish thing to do, and Ahab pretended not to notice how Jezebel happened to be successful at getting his prized land. The king couldn't have such a nasty thing on his conscience. Jezebel rationalized by saying that a king should have what he wanted. Ah, the power of a woman, both for good and for evil. If I had two words to describe Jezebel, I would call her the <u>great manipulator</u>. Keep this in mind: if you find yourself manipulating circumstances, people, events, or ideas to suit your own end, then you know whose company you are in.

1 Kings 21:4–8 And Ahab came into his house heavy and displeased because of the word which Naboth the Jezreelite had spoken to him: for he had said, I will not give thee the inheritance of my fathers. And he laid him down upon his bed, and turned away his face, and would eat no bread.

But Jezebel his wife came to him, and said unto him, Why is thy spirit so sad, that thou eatest no bread?

And he said unto her, Because I spake unto Naboth the Jezreelite, and said unto him, Give me thy vineyard for money; or else, if it please thee, I will give thee another vineyard for it: and he answered, I will not give thee my vineyard.

And Jezebel his wife said unto him, Dost thou now govern the kingdom of Israel? arise, and eat bread, and let thine heart be merry: I will give thee the vineyard of Naboth the Jezreelite.

So she wrote letters in Ahab's name, and sealed them with his seal, and sent the letters unto the elders and to the nobles that were in his city, dwelling with Naboth.

Jezebel provided for her man's wants, but her actions made him weak. Through her the whole nation was opened to judgment. This demonstrates the power an evil woman can have.

If you find yourself saying, "My husband wants it that way," or "My husband doesn't like that," when indeed he has not spoken, then you are a manipulator, using his authority to get your own way.

Self-Righteous Liars

There is another example given to us in Acts chapter 5. A couple, Ananias and Sapphira, decided to sell a piece of property and give the money to aid the needy in the church.

Acts 5:1-10 But a certain man named Ananias <u>with</u> Sapphira his wife, sold a possession,

and <u>kept back</u> part of the price, his wife also being <u>privy</u> to it, and brought a certain part, and laid it at the apostles' feet.

But Peter said, Ananias, why hath Satan filled thine heart to lie to the Holy Ghost, and to keep back part of the price of the land?

Whiles it remained, was it not thine own? and after it was sold, was it not in thine own power? why hast thou conceived this thing in thine heart? thou hast not lied unto men, but unto God.

And Ananias hearing these words fell down, and gave up the ghost: and great fear came on all them that heard these things.

And the young men arose, wound him up, and carried him out, and buried him.

And it was about the space of three hours after, when his wife, not knowing what was done, came in.

And Peter answered unto her, Tell me whether ye sold the land for so much? And she said, Yea, for so much.

Then Peter said unto her, <u>How is it that ye have agreed together to tempt the Spirit of the Lord?</u> behold, the feet of them which have buried thy husband are at the door, and shall carry thee out.

Then fell she down straightway at his feet, and yielded up the ghost: and the young men came in, and found her dead, and carrying her forth, buried her by her husband.

God knows our hearts. Sapphira could have simply answered Peter with: "Ask my husband."

Behind Every Great Man Is...

Proverbs 31 reveals the woman of honor and strength. When a woman steps up to reverence her husband, she can be a more powerful, a more influential woman for good than Jezebel was for bad. God, who made man, knows the best way to motivate a man to achieve greatness. The instructions we find in the Bible show us a powerful woman who stands with her man, motivating him with reverence, prayer, encouragement, and help. When a woman does this....Oh, what a man can do with support like that!

I would like to sanctify this old proverb and say it this way,

Behind every great man is a hidden woman.

<u>A hidden woman is there like an angel, ministering and helping him</u>. She isn't out front or pushing him out the door. She is there, constant and strong. She isn't manipulating things to fit her conscience or will, but is trusting God to direct her man. The influence of a hidden woman is powerful, although it is behind the

scenes. She encourages him and blesses him. She can strengthen him and give him courage in so many situations. If you don't take anything away from this message except one thing, then let it be this: <u>amazing things happen inside of a man when his wife believes in him and honors him.</u>

Praying for your husband is placing him in God's hands. As a woman, you do not personally have the power to make your husband great, or good, or even confident. The Spirit of God can do all of these things. It is important as you speak encouragement to your husband that you avoid:

1. Being like Jezebel, who helped Ahab be a wimp by treating him like a small boy, defending him, and pandering to his whining (I Kings 21).

2. Being like Sapphira, who joined in her husband's lie to the Spirit of God and ended up in the grave beside him (Acts 5).

3. Being like Eve, who influenced Adam to disobey God by tempting him to do what God had commanded him not to do (Genesis 3:6).

Your husband is responsible for his own actions, and you are responsible for yours. However, you should make sure you are not a part of his problem. Make sure you are pure in speech and actions toward him. If you feel he is weak in an area, then pray. Pray with all your heart and soul that God would deliver him. The Almighty God is the great Deliverer.

Chapter Four

A Force to be
Reckoned With

Dearest Wife, *(a letter from a young friend)*
Six months have well-nigh passed since
our sacred union; six of the fullest of my
time on the earth. I have never known
such quality and purpose of life as I have
found in living with a beautiful, kind, intelligent, helpful, and godly woman as my
dear wife. (I love to say "my wife") Sweetheart, you have taught me things I didn't
know were to be learned, and for which life
is fuller and better.

You have loved me well, which is hard to believe. You have not only endured my silliness and immaturity, but have laughed with me, and accepted me fully. You place no conditions on your love, which is priceless. You are loyal, and your heart is pure. You have vision and understanding of the Lord Jesus, and his body, of which I did not see and appreciate heretofore. Your service to Christ is of high repute. Your love for the saints goes before and behind you. I have gained fame and reputation simply by being your husband. It is a joy and honor of immense proportions for me to call you mine.

What else shall I say? Time faileth me to express all that is to be said pertaining to your worth. Suffice me to quote a sage of old, who knew a few things about love:

> **Song of Solomon 4:9,10 Thou hast ravished my heart, my sister, my spouse; thou hast ravished my heart with one of thine eyes, with one chain of thy neck. How fair is thy love, my sister, my spouse! how much better is thy love than wine.**

She Let Him Be

The Story of Mr. and Mrs. J. Frank & Lillian Norris

When I think of a hidden woman, I think of the illustration of John Frank Norris, a Baptist preacher who lived and preached during the 1950s. He was a powerful man and a very influential preacher. He pastored two churches at the same time, one in Fort Worth, Texas, and one in Detroit, Michigan. He flew back and forth, one week in this church, the next in the other.

Earlier, in the 1930s, Brother Norris was just a young preacher who kept struggling and failing. He had many, many needs in his life. Although he labored, it seemed no souls were being saved. His ministry was lame and few were interested in hearing anything he had to say. He was depressed and discouraged. In his heart he would say, "I am going to quit."

His young wife saw that he was struggling. She sensed that he had a need for the power of God. Instead of sitting him down and telling him what a dud he was or what he should preach that wouldn't be quite so dry and boring, this dear lady decided she would fast and pray for her husband. She set aside three days to fast and pray while her husband was away for some meetings. You will notice that this young wife let her husband go out of town to minister. This was the first thing she did—let him be what God had called him to be.

What this lady didn't know was that in her husband's heart these were the last meetings he ever intended to preach. She didn't have any idea that he had said in his heart, "This is it. I'm giving up. I'm done. I'm a flop. I'm no good at this thing, so I'm going to quit. After these meetings, I'm done."

Well, during the last night of those meetings, Brother Norris stood up to preach and suddenly something happened to him that had never happened before. The Spirit of the Most High came upon him and he preached like he had never preached before. He preached with power and conviction knowing that God was upon him and had a message for him to deliver. It was a night to remember. The most hardened sinner in the whole community was sitting in the back row of the church building that night. He came down the aisle weeping and repented toward God. Someone else was there and saw the miracle of that man's conversion, and he also came forward to pray and repent. Before Norris knew what was happening, pandemonium broke out in the building and revival took place. People were weeping and laughing, repenting and praising God. It was a glorious moment for eternity.

Norris excitedly called his wife the next morning. He said, "Honey, you won't believe what is going on here and what happened last night!"

He began to tell the story to his praying wife, and she said, "Oh, praise God! God is so good. Thank you, Jesus." *Brother Norris would never be the same lame preacher again. He had tasted what God wanted for him to do, and he would be a willing vessel. His praying wife was at home with the little ones. She was the hidden woman believing in him when he had almost lost hope in what he had been called to do. Thank God for Mrs. Norris. Thousands of people will stand before the throne someday giving praise to God who were saved through the preaching of this man who almost quit. Don't ever underestimate what God can do if you pray.*

A Stabilizing Influence
Mr. and Mrs. D. L. & Emma Moody

D. L. Moody was another powerful man of God who had a major influence for God during his ministry. Moody had his darling Emma who traveled with him, teaching the children on the road and setting up housekeeping dozens of times during his evangelistic ministry. According to him, she was one of the most stabilizing influences in his life. She was full of grace and kindness. Her example may have motivated the great evangelist to become a compassionate winner of many souls. Who is going to get the glory someday?

He Knew He Had an Advocate
Mr. and Mrs. John & Elizabeth Bunyan

Most all of us have read or at least heard of the book *Pilgrim's Progress*. It was written in 1678. Do you know of any other books that were written that long ago and are still widely read? Did you know John Bunyan was in prison when he wrote it? John Bunyan was blessed with his wife Elizabeth who believed in her husband's confidence to stand firm. She prayed for him and remained in loyal support while he was locked up in jail for twelve long years. She cared for his five children, one of them blind, and visited him in jail faithfully. She never tempted him to compromise so he could come home and help her support the family. Only eternity will reveal the role she played in the writing of *Pilgrim's Progress*. She was a hidden woman who will one day be made known.

Elizabeth Bunyan pleads for her husband before Judge Hale.

A Constant Source of Encouragement

Mr. and Mrs. Robert & Mary Moffat

Robert Moffat had his wife Mary, who sacrificially established his household in a mud hut surrounded by a jungle. Her faith in God and her confidence in Robert became a continual source of encouragement to him.

This was in 1820 when pioneer missionary life was very difficult. Hard times and living in such a primitive and dangerous place didn't prompt Mary to give up. She aided her husband, and together they established one of the most effective mission stations for hundreds of miles around.

Though my situation may be despicable and mean indeed in the eyes of the world, I feel an honour conferred upon me which the highest of the kings of the earth could not have done me; and add to this seeing my dear husband panting for the salvation of the people with unabated ardour, firmly resolving to direct every talent which God has given him to their good and his glory. I am happy, remarkably happy, though the present place of my habitation is a single vestry-room, with a mud wall and a mud floor.
—Mary Moffat, in a letter to her parents, April 8, 1820

For the Eternal Calling

Mr. and Mrs. Adoniram & Ann Judson

Adoniram Judson had his help meet, Ann. Ann was the first of Adoniram's three missionary wives and the most famous one. Together they were pioneer missionaries in the country of Burma, which is in the area of the world near Thailand. They endured many hardships in order to plant the first church of believers in Burma. She was wife, mother, translator, and servant to her husband while he lay in prison for two years. It is hard to imagine the role of a missionary wife. She gave not only her support to her husband, she gave her life in the service of the King of Kings, the Lord Jesus.

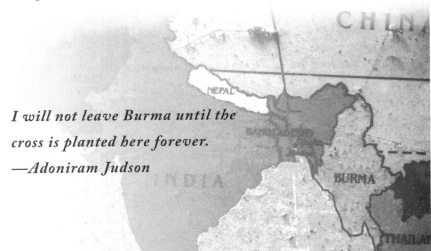

I will not leave Burma until the cross is planted here forever.
—Adoniram Judson

A letter from Adoniram Judson to his future father-in-law

"I have now to ask whether you can consent to part with your daughter early next spring, to see her no more in this world? Whether you can consent to her departure to a heathen land, and her subjection to the hardships and sufferings of a missionary life? Whether you can consent to her exposure to the dangers of the ocean; to the fatal influence of the southern climate of India; to every kind of want and distress; to degradation, insult, persecution, and perhaps a violent death? Can you consent to all this, for the sake of Him who left His heavenly home and died for her and for you; for the sake of perishing, immortal souls; for the sake of Zion and the glory of God? Can you consent to all this, in hope of soon meeting your daughter in the world of glory, with a crown of righteousness brightened by the acclamations of praise which shall resound to her Saviour from heathens saved, through her means, from eternal woe and despair?"

A. Judson

43

Silent Strength

You can see why these men are well known: they had the strength of a hidden woman giving them the help they needed to stay faithful and strong. These women's husbands faced many hardships and dangers in the work of spreading the good news, and each wife suffered terrible adversities. Yet they saw an eternal calling just like their husbands did. Each was a hidden woman who honored God by honoring her man. The smiling face of a wife is priceless!

Plain Old Joe

It is not meant that all men should rise to a place of prominence and be recorded in the pages of history. They will not be leaders in the church or make an impact outside their circle of acquaintances and their family. And that is as it should be. The world needs brick layers, carpenters, and clothes makers. It was such men that God filled with the Holy Spirit so as to do their best work on the temple (Exodus 28:3; 31:3). The Bible never recorded their names, but God knows them and they lived a life with the satisfaction that they performed their common labor in an uncommon and commendable way. "And whatsoever ye do, do it heartily, as to the Lord, and not unto men" (Colossians 3:23). These men were hard working laborers and yet they were doing

God's work. Each man has his gifts and abilities. So many men that would have been Spirit filled brick laborers, blessing their homes and those with whom they work, are ruined by their wife's ambition for them to be something other than their gifts. No amount of praying or wishing will make a man become someone other than whom God calls him to be. A wife is to be a helper to her man. It is his gifts and interest that define the area in which she needs to be a helper.

Many years ago I knew a young fellow who had very few gifts or abilities, being raised by an abusive, mean father. But he met and married a talented, beautiful, very young girl who was looking to leave home as soon as possible, otherwise she would not have married him. Their first years of marriage were terrible, but then the young girl truly came to know the Savior. As she read the Bible she came to see that honor and reverence to her husband would bring glory to God. Anyone knowing her husband would feel her obedience and honor to him would be supernatural, for it was so great a sacrifice and so unwarranted by his actions and demanor.

No amount of praying or wishing will make a man become someone other than whom God calls him to be.

Yet, this girl loved the LORD her God and above all wanted to be doing his work. She knew that as a married woman her work for God would be service to her husband. It was clear that even if the man did get wonderfully saved, he would never be a preacher or teacher, or ever be capable of making much more than minimal wage. He simply didn't have a high enough intelligence to do much. Plus it was obvious he was mentally and emotional cripple from abuse suffered at his father's hands. This beautiful young woman knew that her honor to her husband was her Lord's will and her husband's only hope. She poured into him, telling him every day as he walked in the door from working in the factory that he was a fine, hard-working man. She kissed him goodbye every morning as he left for work and thanked him for his sacrifice in serving the family. He began to see himself as she did: hard-working, responsible, and dependable. Being human, there were times when she almost lost hope, but God is able. The man knew his wife was a jewel. He heard the men

She knew that as a married woman her work for God would be service to her husband.

at work talking about their mean, lazy wives, but he only had good things to say about his. He knew they thought he was really lucky to have found a faithful woman who stood by him. Over the years he began to treat her with more regard until he came to want to please her. He finally came to know the Savior.

After getting saved he was the same old fellow but now he loved to go to church. He said he loved church for two reasons: he wanted to know more about Jesus, and he loved making his woman who had done him good and not evil all the days of his life so happy.

> **Grandma did more than pray; she obeyed God by honoring and reverencing her husband.**

They are old now with many grandchildren and great grandchildren. The children love going fishing and building things with their gentle, kind, patient grandfather. They are safe with him as he is not the angry broken man he once was, nor is he the evil man that his father was. None of the family knows it was Grandma's honor and reverence to Grandfather that broke the devil's chains in that family, they only know that their family is different from the extended family. Grandma's babies are educated, happy, resourceful, and are raising up their children to know and love the Lord. Grandma did more than pray; she obeyed God by honoring and reverencing her husband. Her story is not recorded in the pages of history; it was recorded in the pages of in my life. I knew the nasty evil old father that hurt his young children. I saw the brokenness of the sons and daughters and even grandchildren. When the young wife first came to me, a young preacher's wife for help I had never counseled anyone. Her obedience to God to honor and reverence her husband built faith in me giving me courage and confidence. I saw that God was surely able. Today, now almost 50 years later, millions of wives read my books that teach them how to have glorious marriages by honoring and reverencing their husbands. I learned first from this young girl.

A Simple Prayer Opened the Doors of Heaven

Mr. and Mrs. Denny & Jackie Kenaston

(the author's own story)

Oh, the power of a support unit in the midst of spiritual warfare! There was a day when the battle was raging over these teachings. I wanted to preach the message to the husbands and then a message to wives, but my voice was failing me. No one knew about the physical struggle I was going through except for a very few who we had been praying with. I was in the middle of a very intense prayer meeting where men and women were crying out to God with fervency. The place was alive with prayer and thanksgiving.

My wife could not get into the room because it was so packed with people. She wasn't there. Then God said to me, "Get up! Go find your wife and ask her to pray for you." I got up and made my way through the press of all the people and found my dear wife. I got on my knees in my little study. She laid her hands on me and prayed. As she cried out to God for me, heaven came down. I knelt there and wept like a baby. I knew God heard, I felt my strength return. God cleared my voice so I could teach that night. All of those prayer warriors down on their knees in the prayer room couldn't break through the clouds that were over me, but the simple prayer of my sweet wife opened the doors of heaven over my heart and mind. I needed her to be my prayer warrior. *Your husband needs you to pray for him. Every husband needs to feel that his wife is there standing with him. A man is the most vulnerable with his wife. A woman has power over her man. Oh, that she would use that power to pray and support him to do what God has called him to do!*

Don't ever underestimate what God can do if you pray.

For the word of God is quick, and powerful, and sharper than any twoedged sword, piercing even to the dividing asunder of soul and spirit, and of the joints and marrow, and is a discerner of the thoughts and intents of the heart.
Hebrews 4:12

Chapter Five

Let's Be
Honest

**Reverence can encourage your husband
so that God can make him into a godly man.**

I have received many letters from women saying, "I want this life that you speak about. I hear what you are saying and I want to help my husband. How can I help him? He just does not care about his responsibilities before God."

Most times it is easy to read between the lines of those letters and see that the woman is really saying, "I am sick of this guy and the way he is. Can you please tell me how to change him?"

No, I cannot tell you how to change him. But if you want to know how you can be an encouragement to that man, I can tell you that. God does not bless sanctified manipulation sisters. Write that one down. Manipulation, any way you paint it, will never be blessed of the Spirit of God. I think Eve was manipulating when she ate the fruit. She knew Adam was not touching the fruit but she was convinced it would make both of them wiser, so she took it and gave it to her husband. If you lay down any sin as a wife, let it be that of manipulating your husband.

God does not bless sanctified manipulation.

If you are a young sister yet unmarried then you need to purpose in your heart to avoid manipulating anyone for anything, be it younger brothers or sisters or friends or parents. What you are as a single young woman is what you will be as a married woman. Do not practice manipulating people or circumstances to suit your convictions. All people dislike being manipulated, but husbands really resist it and find women who do it repulsive. Rather than manipulating, try using what God told wives to use: reverence.

Reverence

Reverence can encourage your husband so that God can make him into a godly man.

Ephesians 5:33... and the wife see that she reverence her husband.

Let's look at the word *reverence*. Reverence is one of the most motivating, effectual qualities in human relationships. It can flow from a woman to a man, and even from a man to a man. I am going to go through a list of words that are used to describe reverence.

Fear

There is a shocking definition out of Webster's 1828 Dictionary on the word *reverence*. The first definition is usually the most definitive.

Fear: to reverence someone is to fear them.

This may cause the modern woman to cry out in opposition. "Fear? I'm not going to fear my husband!" Yet, even the dictionary describes reverence as "fear, mingled with respect and affection."

Why should you fear your husband?

When the world looks on and sees you reverencing your husband as you would Christ, and your husband loving and caring for you as Christ loved the Church, they see a picture of Christ and the Church. Paul calls it a "mystery." Your fear of your husband is an example of how humanity should fear and obey God. Not in terror of his evil, for God is good, but in real fear of losing his favor, protection, and provision. This godly fear is recognition of God's position and power.

To fear your husband is to demonstrate the same awareness that your husband is responsible for your well-being and that you rest in his hands. You are at the same time demonstrating your fear of God. What a testimony you can have!

> **Ephesians 5:32–33 This is a great mystery: but I speak concerning Christ and the church. Nevertheless let every one of you in particular so love his wife even as himself; and the wife see that she reverence her husband.**

♡ Submit

If you reverence someone, you will submit to him. The word *submit* means to yield or surrender to the power, will, or authority of another. *Submit* goes one step further than *obey*. Obedience can be done as an outward act, but submission requires an inward attitude of surrender with obedience. This is beautiful to God. Submission is what Christ demonstrated in his relationship with his Father while he walked the earth.

As Jesus knelt in the garden praying before his crucifixion, he was in great distress over the path ahead of him, the path his Father was leading him down. Yet he prayed in submission:

> **Luke 22:42 Saying, Father, if thou be willing, remove this cup**

from me: nevertheless not my will, but thine, be done.

The Bible teaches that a woman should submit to her husband "as unto the Lord." Is this because he is as good as Christ? No. It is because Jesus is good; submitting to him makes sense.

> **Ephesians 5:22 Wives, submit yourselves unto your own husbands, as unto the Lord.**

Colossians 3:18 Wives, submit yourselves unto your own husbands, as it is fit in the Lord.

 *Regard*

Reverence also includes *attention*.

Yes, notice your husband. Pay attention to what he says. Pay attention to what he is feeling. Observe him with the eyes and consider him with your mind. The act by which we gain knowledge of someone is to focus on them. Turn your eyes upon your husband with attentive interest in what he is doing. *A man knows when his wife is avoiding looking at him. It is an act of rebellion, disinterest, and shows that you do not reverence him. It is the opposite of what God calls you to do and be toward your husband.* Your man should feel your interested eyes looking at him when he is around. He should know that you are considering his needs so that you might meet them.

> **Psalms 102:17 He will regard the prayer of the destitute, and not despise their prayer.**

How can you reverence someone whom you do not regard? *Regard* means "to give focused attention and to consider seriously." When you regard something, you give it value. If you want your husband to be a leader, then be quiet and listen to him when he speaks. Look attentively at the things that he says and consider them. He will talk more. He will lead more. He will rise up to his responsibilities and be a man. *Small attitudes often break or make a marriage. This is one of those simple cures that bring great healing.*

❤ Honor

Included in reverence is honor: "the outward expression of respect or high esteem by your words or actions." It can also mean "to adorn, ornament, and decorate something or someone." This is the same word used to describe "honoring the king." It is also what happens when a war hero is decorated or honored.

Honor your husband with your words and actions. You will never be sorry that you did.

❤ Prefer

Reverencing your husband also means that you will prefer him. The word *prefer* means "to bear or carry in advance, to consider one to be better than you are." In practical language it means to place his desires, opinions, and ideas ahead of your own. You can't imagine the confidence that this builds in a man when he senses from the depth of your heart that you are more interested in what he thinks than what you think.

Prefer also means to yield to another's opinion or judgment because of respect and honor. This is the most beautiful quality a wife can have. She can display this confidence builder often, as there are always a lot of opinions in marriage.

Some men are interested in a bilateral conversation with real input from their wives. It is important to discover what your husband prefers—even in your relationship with him. If he wants your real opinion and you just nod and repeat his own words back to him, that could be irritating. Above all, find out who your man is and prefer his idea of good communication.

> *Let him be a man before God, not a would-be man before you.*

♡ Esteem

Only God deserves worship, but when a man senses that his wife values him, what he does, and what he says, it affects his leadership ability tremendously. You can't imagine how much this will strengthen him. To esteem someone is "to prize or set high value on" them. Do you have a high opinion of your husband? Have you given him a high place of honor in your mind, words, and actions? That is esteem.

Ultimately, what I'm saying is, let him go. Let him be a man before God, not a would-be man before you. He'll be fired up to

do what he's supposed to do if he senses freedom and uncondi-
tional reverence coming out of your heart. Prefer and venerate
him. Give him worth and respect. Do you esteem what God says
about your attitude toward your husband? In Psalms, God reminds
us to esteem his precepts, which are his teachings.

> **Psalms 119:128 Therefore I esteem all thy precepts concerning
> all things to be right; and I hate every false way.**

 *Praise*

To *praise* is to "value with words." To lift or raise another with
words of value and gratitude. This word is a good outward expression of many of the words we've already gone over. If you have the
attitude of honor, you will praise your husband with your words. If
he has your attention, then you will see when he does something
great and respond with praise. Praise is like fuel on the fire of your
husband's heart. He will do things you never dreamed he could do.

*The word praise appears 192 times in Scripture.
Praise is not a feeling, attitude, or a point of worship.
Praise is an act. It is doing something. Praise is saying thank you, singing of your appreciation, lifting
up your hand in thanksgiving, or playing a musical
instrument while considering your appreciation of the
Lord. Praise is an act of obedience.*

> **Psalms 51:15 O Lord, open thou my lips; and my mouth shall
> shew forth thy praise.**

Psalms 54:6 I will freely sacrifice unto thee: I will praise thy name, O LORD; for it is good.

Psalms 56:10 In God will I praise his word: in the LORD will I praise his word.

♡ *Love*

Love is "a prompt, free, willing desire for someone. It is to be pleased with and regard with strong affection. Love is ardent fellowship, springing from high esteem, a word of endearment." The love of a woman is without question the strongest motivation in a man's life. It will cause him to do and become far greater than you ever thought he could do or become. Look at the love of a man for a woman he wants to marry, a woman who loves him in return. Look at what he will go through for her. He'll go through anything!

♡ *Admire*

Lastly, to reverence someone is to admire them exceedingly. To *admire* means "to hold up, to stop and behold with wonder. To

Does your husband feel your admiration?

regard with strong affection, a pleasant respect with wonder." Does your husband feel your admiration? You might have admired him more before you married him than you do now. Regain that admiration. Remember the things about him that impressed you long ago and admire him once again.

What Will You Do?

Ephesians 5:33 ...and the wife see that she reverence her husband.

I have given you a list of words that describe the act of reverencing. There are three ways you can respond to this list that you've just been given.

You can be careless and indifferent and pass it off with little interest. Remember that Jezebel was raised carelessly.

You can be overwhelmed by it and give up in discouragement. (Don't listen to Satan! God says to stand!)

You can be stirred, motivated, and convicted by it. You can rise up in faith with a will to do as God has directed you. (Write down your commitment so that you can reread it every week.)

I pray that you will do the latter with vision and purpose in your heart from this day forward. All of the principles of the Bible are effectual. They work; they have an effect. If you drop a stone in a pond, the ripples from that rock go on and on. Your obedience to God will affect your life, your husband, your children, and your friends, possibly for generations to come. This is the law of sowing and reaping. If you choose to reverence your husband, you will receive a bountiful harvest.

The opposite is also true; we cannot escape the principle of sowing and reaping. God Almighty, the Creator, has set in motion these laws of cause and effect and has given you power to reap a good harvest or a bad one. Your husband can be known as the man who sits in the gates (Proverbs 31) or the man who lies in bed with his face to the wall (Ahab). Which kind of husband do you want? The Proverbs 31 lady who is so well acclaimed as being a woman of great price has the privilege of having her husband in a high position. God gives us this piece of information in the middle of telling how the good woman spends her day. It would appear that God is saying that her lifestyle makes it possible for him to get to the top.

Proverbs 31:23 Her husband is known in the gates, when he sitteth among the elders of the land.

The love of a woman is without question the strongest motivation in a man's life.

Proverbs 31

Who can find a virtuous woman? for her price is far above rubies.

The heart of her husband doth safely trust in her, so that he shall have no need of spoil.

She will do him good and not evil all the days of her life.

She seeketh wool, and flax, and worketh willingly with her hands.

She is like the merchants' ships; she bringeth her food from afar.

She riseth also while it is yet night, and giveth meat to her household, and a portion to her maidens.

She considereth a field, and buyeth it: with the fruit of her hands she planteth a vineyard.

She girdeth her loins with strength, and strengtheneth her arms.

She perceiveth that her merchandise is good: her candle goeth not out by night.

She layeth her hands to the spindle, and her hands hold the distaff.

She stretcheth out her hand to the poor; yea, she reacheth forth her hands to the needy.

She is not afraid of the snow for her household: for all her household are clothed with scarlet.

She maketh herself coverings of tapestry; her clothing is silk and purple.

Her husband is known in the gates, when he sitteth among the elders of the land.

She maketh fine linen, and selleth it; and delivereth girdles unto the merchant.

Strength and honour are her clothing; and she shall rejoice in time to come.

She openeth her mouth with wisdom; and in her tongue is the law of kindness.

She looketh well to the ways of her household, and eateth not the bread of idleness.

Her children arise up, and call her blessed; her husband also, and he praiseth her.

Many daughters have done virtuously, but thou excellest them all.

Favour is deceitful, and beauty is vain: but a woman that feareth the LORD, she shall be praised.

Give her of the fruit of her hands; and let her own works praise her in the gates.

"[Before we were married, my mother] wisely reasoned that my chosen husband was no ordinary man, that his whole life was absolutely dedicated to God and His service, and that I must never, never hinder him by trying to put myself first in his heart."
—*Susannah Spurgeon*

Chapter Six

How to Make Your Husband Weak

**Do you remember who your enemy is?
Not your husband, not even your flesh,
not your circumstances or money problems.**

Here is how to make your husband into a weak and timid man, one who sits in the corner and doesn't talk much, one who is afraid to lead in conversation or make decisions, one who will always look to you to see what you think before he speaks. God help us.

*H*ere's what you do: Disregard what he says. Don't notice him when he's around. When he comes home from work, don't greet him. Look the other way when he's talking, or bring up some other subject when he's speaking. Dishonor him; belittle him as you walk through life together. Don't fulfill his desires for the home and family. Push him away and tell him to get out of your way. Find fault with him. Make him feel your ideas are better, smarter, wiser, more clever, and certainly produce a better outcome. Let him feel your silent disapproval. Manipulate circumstances when you think he has made a lesser decision, as it will irritate him and make him just want to quit trying.

I guarantee you, in five years you'll have a husband who will sit in the corner, or you'll have an angry, bitter man who avoids coming home.

Have You Been Lied To?

Do you remember who your enemy is? Not your husband, not even your flesh, not your circumstances or money problems. Your enemy is powers, principalities, and rulers of darkness. This is a war with evil, and the Enemy wants you to stumble, fail, be broken, lose hope, get angry, and stop believing and trusting God. He wants to use you to keep your husband weak. He wants you to question God's WORDS.

> **Ephesians 6:12–14a For we wrestle not against flesh and blood, but against principalities, against powers, against the rulers of the darkness of this world, against spiritual wick-**

edness in high places. Wherefore take unto you the whole armour of God, that ye may be able to withstand in the evil day, and having done all, to stand. Stand therefore...

The devil is a liar. He's been pulling the wool over the eyes of millions of women. Many of them are Christian women. A whole generation of men have been devastated and debilitated by the lies of the devil.

We all make mistakes, both men and women. We men are a generation who didn't have leaders, and now we're trying to be leaders. We want to do what is right, but it takes a little while to learn a new thing, and manhood that is done God's way is an entirely different new thing. I have seen men praying and crying out to God to strength-en them to walk in the new way. They may stumble and fall a few times. They haven't

Do you remember who your enemy is?

seen an example of what being a godly husband and father is supposed to look like. They're figuring it out for the first time. I encourage you to have patience with love and wait for your man to learn to stand, walk, and lead.

A while back I was encouraging a woman to sit through family Bible study with a supportive smile on her face even when she knew her husband was making a mess of what he was trying to do. This reminded me of when we choose a man to become an elder over the body of Christ. *(Elders in this church are chosen by drawing lots, not by gifts.)* At first, the new elder isn't sure of his new role and is a little nervous. He feels he's being watched, and he is. *He is usually boring and we all suffer a little under the long minutes of boredom. He is often reluctant to go ahead with his duties, and he drags his feet so we all have to step up to cover his job. He is learning to lead. He is learning to trust. He is learning his job as a man who is over the flock. It is not easy being put in a position of authority and responsibility.*

That previous list I covered of the words that define reverence comes into play as we support the new elder while he learns his role and gains confidence before God and man. He needs encouragement. He needs an "amen" when he tries, or a pat on the back.

I don't have a godly husband; why should I treat him as though he were godly?

That is his beginning. Two years later that elder is a trusted and effective minister in the Word.

But think a moment about what would become of that new leader if he were treated differently? What if we didn't listen to him when he tried to speak? What if we turned our heads away and frowned at him when he was preaching? *What if we just put our heads down as if we were ashamed?* What if you or someone wrote him a note to tell him that he didn't do too well? What kind of elder do you think he'd be in two years' time? I can tell you that he would either be a puppet (which is no elder at all), or he'd just quit (which is also no elder at all.)

You see, we know these principles when we take them out of the realm of the home and family. We understand how they work to encourage and support someone who we hope will succeed. So, God help us to take this knowledge back into the home. Let me give you some counsel, you wives and daughters. I encourage you to take this list of reverence words and memorize it and internalize it into your heart and soul. Tape it to your refrigerator and refer to it daily. Pray over it and ask God to work it into your heart. Stand against the devil and declare you will honor your man.

If you treat your husband with reverence, how do you think this will affect him? Will it make him a better man or a worse man? Will it encourage him or discourage him? Will he feel good about himself or will he think that he's no good? Do you think he'll be harder on you or more kind to you?

Many times when this message is preached to a mixed group, it is the men that respond the most. If I preach this message to the women and then give an invitation to come forward for prayer, it would be the men that would respond. They'd be weeping at the altar, saying "I don't deserve a wife like that."

Bless your husband, dear sister. Bless him.

Proverbs 31:12 She will do him good and not evil all the days of her life.

Some might say, "I don't have a godly husband; why should I treat him as though he were godly? Isn't that just pretending, which is a form of lying?" This is a legitimate question. Some women are married to men who do not know God in the most fundamental ways. However, the Scripture states:

Ephesians 5:22 Wives, submit yourselves unto your own husbands, as unto the Lord.

God knows your husband isn't perfect. However, if your husband is fulfilling the basic requirements of marriage and is not abusing you or the children, then submit to him as unto the Lord. <u>Don't make the mistake of overstating how bad your man is. You would be falling into the hands of Satan</u>. Surely you fear God's judgment. Let that fear of God translate into obedience and reverence toward your husband.

Imagine that God is a 100-foot bridge you might fall off of and die. Your husband is the guardrail. Crashing through the guardrail won't kill you, but falling off the bridge will. You don't need to pretend that your husband is the bridge (the holy, all-powerful, perfect God); you know that he isn't. But you also know that if you stay aware of him, respect his position, and don't cross him, God will bless you with a safer path—a path that may

God knows your husband isn't perfect.

save your children, and in time, your husband.

If your husband sits on the couch watching movies while you go to work, then praising him for being a great provider is ludicrous. But if he brings home the paycheck and takes you to buy groceries and you fail to thank him and praise him for his care, this is the moment when you might plummet off the side of the bridge.

The Power of a Submissive Spirit

Let's go on now and look at the power of a submissive spirit.

> **1 Peter 3:1–2 Likewise, ye wives, be in subjection to your own husbands; that, if any obey not the word, they also may without the word be won by the conversation of the wives; while they behold your chaste conversation coupled with fear.**

In these verses there is a powerful secret that a discontented woman will never know. You see that Peter says "likewise." He is referring to the example of Christ suffering and dying on the cross. Peter is saying "wives, be like Christ..."

There is also that word *fear* again. You are probably not afraid of your husband. But if you know God, you are afraid of *him*. If you fear God, you will keep his commandments, and he said to reverence your husband. If you fear God, you will reverence your husband.

> **1 Peter 3:3–6 Whose adorning, let it not be that outward adorning of plaiting the hair, and of wearing of gold, or of putting**

on of apparel; but let it be the hidden man of the heart, in that which is not corruptible, even the ornament of a meek and quiet spirit, which is in the sight of God of great price.

For after this manner in the old time the holy women also, who trusted in God, adorned themselves, being in subjection unto their own husbands: Even as Sara obeyed Abraham, calling him lord: whose daughters ye are, as long as ye do well, and are not afraid with any amazement.

We see in these verses God's instruction to a woman who is not married to a believer, or at least one that does not obey the Word of God. There are many women who fall into this category. What are they to do?

Notice that the Proverbs 31 woman is described as being of great price. She is valuable above all else. Her worth is not of what she wears or how finely she fixes herself to look, but of what is in her heart and mind. God calls it an ornament. A Christmas ornament is what is hung on the tree to make it pretty. God says a meek and quiet spirit is an ornament. A quiet spirit is what is found in a woman who is not stirred up to wrath or bitterness. A quiet spirit is a satisfied, thankful spirit—restful, peaceful, content in heart rather than ready to take offense or set a man straight. Many husbands walk on eggshells, worried that they will do something to irritate their wife. And some wives get ticked off if their husband is late to dinner, talks too long after church, forgets to clean his shoes off before coming in the house, or any one of *a dozen odd offenses that men seem often to commit. God calls a quiet spirit an ornament, and all men are profoundly thankful when they have a wife who is content. This ornament stirs a man whether he is lost or saved to want to please his woman. This is a gift to women who are married to lost men. They can show forth a quiet and meek spirit and thereby win their husbands. God says, don't be surprised when your husband is willing to hear the gospel—be not afraid with any amazement. As you have won his heart with your sweet spirit, God can win him.*

God has given significant power to the wife of a man who will not obey God. Real power. Power to win him to God. Just think: how much influence a woman has who is married to a man who has the Spirit of God in him? A man who believes?

Believe this, dear lady. You are a powerhouse of influence in your home when you get into this place that God has designed for you. When you put on this meek and quiet spirit, you are priceless and powerful.

A woman with a submissive spirit adapts to the desires and direction of her husband. As I have studied this portion of Scripture, I am absolutely convinced that this hidden man of the heart that the husband will see in you is Jesus. He is the hidden man of the heart.

That is amazing. Jesus can reach your husband. Do you want your husband to be saved? Put on a meek and quiet spirit and adorn yourself with Jesus.

Godly Examples of Reverence

Mr. and Mrs. Charles & Susannah Spurgeon

Charles Spurgeon is known as one of the greatest among preachers and writers. His pen has taught generations of young men to know and love God's words. But what of his wife?

It is of great interest to know that when Charles was consider-ing Susannah as his wife, that he sent her the book **Pilgrim's Progress** *by John Bunyan. You remember we just learned how John Bunyan's good wife stayed faithful to him even though she suffered greatly due to his standing firm concerning issues of his day and thus was jailed those long years. Even when she struggled to feed the children, she encouraged her husband. And now all these years later God is using the book John wrote to teach and encourage the soon-to-be wife of a man who would teach millions the Word of God. Thank God John's wife had good courage and stood as a woman of great price.*

Charles Spurgeon's wife, Susannah, had many talents and was very intelligent. Among those talents was the ability to read and write Greek and Hebrew! This is a lady who could easily outshine her husband. But they had a beautiful relationship. She had a special name that she called him: Tirshatha. It is the Persian word for "the revered one."

You will find that word in Nehemiah (8:9) where it calls Nehemiah the "Tirshatha."

Can you imagine each morning when Susannah greeted Mr. Spurgeon with the words, "Good morning, my Reverence. How did you sleep last night?"

Susannah's attitude fueled Charles Spurgeon's fire to minister. Most people have no idea what battles he faced in his ministry. He dealt with discouragement and criticism. He suffered greatly from gout from the time he was 30 years old. He was oppressed by many things, but the powerful relationship that he had with his wife was a continual encouragement to him to keep going. Susannah herself was very ill for over 15 years, but she was steadfast in service to and for him. It was her work of translation and preparation for print that got his books into the hands of young preachers so they might learn from Spurgeon. Today Spurgeon's books are still studied by most preachers.

Charles Spurgeon was gone traveling and preaching much of their married life. Their private letters record how they loved one another. In one such letter, Charles wrote to his love saying, "My Own Dear One— None know how grateful I am to God for you. In all I have ever done for Him, you have a large share. For in making me so happy you have fitted me for service. Not an ounce of power has ever been lost to the good cause through you. I have served the Lord far more, and never less, for your sweet companionship. The Lord God Almighty bless you now and forever!"

Charles Spurgeon became the most famous preacher in Victorian England. He founded a pastor's college and an orphanage that still exist today. Many of his books are still in print. What a great loss to heaven and to earth if Spurgeon's wife had not reverenced her husband.

Abraham and Sarah

Sarah spoke to Abraham, calling him lord, or master. To be his wife she had to leave her friends and family and wander around homeless her whole life. Abraham was looking for a city that wasn't there yet, a city whose builder and maker is God. But Sarah wasn't amazed or afraid at this life. She called Abraham lord and followed him through the wilderness.

I wonder how most wives would feel if their husbands said, "I think we should get a tent and start traveling around because I feel there is a city we should be looking for that God wants us to find." And they travel days, weeks, months, and years and yet the husband just can't seem to find what he is looking for. The wife sleeps, cooks, and lives in a tent all her life because she is trusting her husband to do the right thing for her. Clearly God chose a wonderful woman to fill this role as Abraham's wife. She is listed in Hebrews as one of the great men and women who lived by faith.

1 Peter 3:6 Even as Sara obeyed Abraham, calling him lord: whose daughters ye are, as long as ye do well, and are not afraid with any amazement.

76

Hebrews 11:8–11 By faith Abraham, when he was called to go out into a place which he should after receive for an inheritance, obeyed; and he went out, not knowing whither he went.

By faith he sojourned in the land of promise, as in a strange country, dwelling in tabernacles with Isaac and Jacob, the heirs with him of the same promise: For he looked for a city which hath foundations, whose builder and maker is God.

Through faith also Sara herself received strength to conceive seed, and was delivered of a child when she was past age, because she judged him faithful who had promised.

It is the spirit behind these ladies that I'm looking at here. It's not that one name is holier than the other—it's that these women reverenced their husbands, even with their terms of endearment.

When Sarah spoke to Abraham, calling him lord, she had all the power of all those attitudes of reverence that I gave you earlier. She was saying to her husband, "I love you. I highly esteem you. I care about what you say. I'm glad to be under your authority. I belong to you. I'm here for you, and you are all I want."

If you are a better Christian than your husband, then the best way to prove it is by obeying God's plain commands concerning him and the home.
—*John R. Rice,*
Rebellious Wives and Slacker Husbands

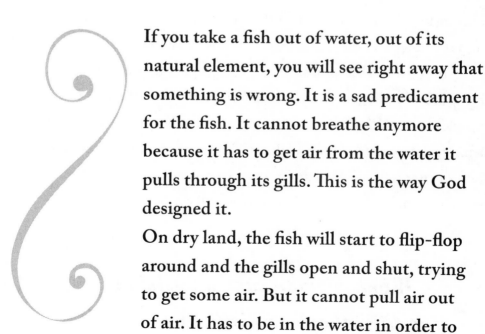

Chapter Seven

Fish Out of Water

Females were not created to be in a man's place; they can't make it there and still be a lady.

If you take a fish out of water, out of its natural element, you will see right away that something is wrong. It is a sad predicament for the fish. It cannot breathe anymore because it has to get air from the water it pulls through its gills. This is the way God designed it.

On dry land, the fish will start to flip-flop around and the gills open and shut, trying to get some air. But it cannot pull air out of air. It has to be in the water in order to breathe.

*M*any ladies are like the fish out of water. They have set their hearts on being somewhere other than the place God designed for them when he created the first lady. Females were not created to be in a man's place; they can't make it there and still be a lady. It's a different habitat, an element they were not designed for.

Some women say, "I will not stand in the place which God made for women. I am going to do my own thing somewhere else. I'm going to be on my own. I am not going to stay home and take care of babies and serve my husband. Let him stay home and wash dishes."

When women take a position like this, they are fish out of water and they are gasping for air but not breathing.

As soon as you drop a fish back into the water, everything is okay again. Oxygen comes with the water through the gills and into the lungs and the fish is fine. It swims away, relieved.

Are you a fish out of water? Are you gasping for air, for every bit of life you can get? Are you wondering why everything is so upside-down? Why you are so frustrated, have hormonal problems, feel depressed or overworked? Maybe you need to jump back into the water of God's plan for you. His purpose for you as a woman is the most natural element you will ever know.

When women take a position like this, they are fish out of water.

The Story of Jane

When I was in Bible school many years ago, I knew a dear sister named Jane. She was single, and there were a lot of single girls there in the school. They were studying to be teachers in a Christian school.

As I look back to those days, I can see that this young woman was practicing giving honor to those in authority. She was practicing how she would honor and encourage her husband when God gave her a man.

My job was the bus ministry. At the time it was work, but now I am glad for it because it changed my life. As I was working in the bus ministry, this one young lady really stood out, head and shoulders above the rest.

Jane had this whole honor thing down. She would write notes and let me know that she was praying for me. I was not special to her—just a leader. She did the same thing for the pastor of the church and some others. She was that amazing "support unit" I talked about earlier.

The pastor would get a note from Jane saying "I'm praying for you today. I'm behind you. God bless you today. I thought about you this morning, so I'm praying for you."

I started to get notes like this all the time and I thought to myself, "Man, somebody better open up his eyes and get ahold of that girl. She is going to make some man a beautiful wife someday!"

I know exactly what happened to that fellow

A lot of fellows passed her by. She wasn't the prettiest girl in the school. She didn't stand out as anything special. I wanted to tell the single guys, "Hey, you're looking with the wrong set of glasses. This girl's price is far above rubies!" The guys passed her by for the flip-flopping girls. And they got what they asked for—they got a flip-flop.

One day Jane came to me for counsel. She said "Brother, I need your help. I have a young man who is asking to court me."

In our Bible school if someone wanted to court you, it meant they were strongly considering marrying you. So I knew this was serious. She gave me the name of the young man and said, "I want to know what you think."

I did my investigation and checked the fellow out. He was a fine young man, and I had no doubt about that. But I thought to myself that he was just so-so. Not a dynamic leader or a powerful preacher. He was kind of a slow starter, and I thought he would never amount to anything in the ministry or even as a church member. He was just a good guy. I thought, "Poor Jane. What a shame that such a go-getter gal would be lost to the ministry with this fellow. You could do much better than this guy."

But I didn't tell her that. I had found out that he was a good guy, and so what else should I say? So I told her, "He seems to be a very nice young man. If you feel like God is leading you, go ahead and go that way."

They courted, married, and guess what she did? All those notes and prayers, all those encouraging words and good cheer, she turned them loose on that young man who I had thought was just "so-so."

In two years' time he was one of the finest leaders in the Bible college. I just shook my head in amazement and smiled—the power of a reverencing woman is more than anyone could ever know. You had to see it to believe it was possible.

I heard people saying, "Who is that new preacher? He is really dramatic!" And I told them, "Oh, he is not new. He has been here for three years. His name is so-and-so. Remember him?" And the response was always the same: "Really? I sorta remember him, but wow, has he come out!" It was clear that people thought, "What happened to him? He must have been a late bloomer."

I knew what happened to him. I knew exactly what happened to that fellow. He got ahold of that dear lady who believed in him, prayed for him, saw in him what wasn't there yet but could be,

Something started burning inside of that "so-so" guy and he turned into a mighty man of God.

encouraged and blessed him, and loved and admired him. Then all of a sudden something started burning inside of that "so-so" guy and he turned into a mighty man of God.

Praise God for his wisdom and bless his name!

You ladies have as much power available to you as Jane did. You can bless and influence your husbands just as she blessed and influenced her man.

More About Jane

I (Debi Pearl) read this story and loved it. But personally, as a woman, if a young, attractive girl had been sending my husband notes of encouragement, it would have alarmed me. If a married woman had been sending my husband notes of encouragement, it would have highly alarmed me. I am sure most women would share this sentiment. Marriage is sacred. Let me say again, marriage is sacred. Anything that could cause insecurity in someone's marriage, whether it is good or bad, should always be avoided. Being a man, Denny would not have understood the psychic of most wives concerning these notes. Denny found these notes to be an encouragement. But we don't know how these notes might have affected some of the pastors' wives. In the end, one note of "encouragement" could have been an instrument in bringing discord in marriage. Now, I would like to clarify this issue to you: if you are single, your father and your brothers are the men in your life who need your encouragement and honor. I trained my daughters to show respect and encouragement to their brothers, which in turn trained them in how they treat their husbands. It made their brothers protective of their sisters, and caused them to be better men. Certainly you need to pray for your pastors and leaders, but any notes should be addressed to "Mr. and Mrs." As a preacher's wife for going on 50 years, I greatly appreciate it when I receive a note of encouragement and respect from a younger woman.

In this book we have read amazing stories of preachers and missionaries who God greatly used. The thing all of these mighty men of God had in common was a strong, virtuous, reverent wife who was not only willing, but gladly supported him in whatever call God gave him. Jane should have sent her notes of encouragement to the wife rather than the husband.

Papa's Chair

Ephesians 5:22 Wives, submit yourselves unto your own husbands, as unto the Lord.

This is a powerful statement. It doesn't just tell the woman to submit to her husband, it says "as unto the Lord."

Almost every home has a chair or two in it that the daddy sits in. It's his chair. I have one that I sit in at my house. In fact, I think I have two of them. It's called "Papa's chair." If Papa's around or if he walks into the room, the kids all scatter out of that chair. It's Papa's chair, and they know it.

I want you to imagine a situation in order to illustrate Ephesians 5:22 to you:

Picture the chair your husband sits in when he comes into your home in the evening. You know the scene; it happens all the time. He comes in, maybe home from work, and he goes and sits in that chair.

Now, instead of your husband walking in the door, greeting everyone, and then sitting down in his chair to visit with you, I want you to picture this time, instead of your husband, it's the Lord Jesus Christ. He just walks through the door of your house, gives everyone a warm greeting, crosses the floor, and sits down in the chair.

Jesus sits there as though he feels right at home and has sat there many times. Wow! What an exciting experience! The Lord Jesus Christ is sitting in your house. What are you going to do next? What will be your response?

We can easily imagine what is going on in your heart and mind at this point, thoughts of reverence and delight. You think, "What should I do to serve my Lord? He is sitting in my house where my husband usually sits. What should I do to please him?"

Imagine it. You say "Lord, is there anything that I can get you? Is there anything you would like right now?"

Jesus says, "Yes, I would like a cup of tea."

You say, "Yes, my Lord. What kind of tea would you like?"

"I think I'll have some mint tea," he says.

"Yes, Lord, right away. I'll make it right now. Would you like honey in it? How much honey?"

You go back to the kitchen thinking, "Oh, glory! Jesus is in my house and I am serving him tea! Hallelujah, oh my, oh my! I am going to make tea for Jesus Christ! What a privilege."

You would be so excited to make that cup of tea. It will be the best cup of tea you ever made. Why? Because it is for the Lord!

When the tea is ready for him, you joyfully serve it to him. I doubt you would quickly walk away like many other times before. No, the Lord is sitting in that chair. You will place the tea in his hand and sit down to look at him. Remember those definitions of *reverence*? Remember the word *regard*?

You will be looking his way to see how the tea is. You will watch him take the first sip.

"Is it too hot? I could get an ice cube to cool it down. Does it taste all right? Is there enough honey it?"

"Oh, yes, it's fine."

Will you walk away? No. The Lord Jesus is sitting in the chair. You want to know what he might say next. You are sitting on the edge of your seat waiting to hear what he is going to say.

You listen to him for a while and then during a pause you say, "Lord, I have supper on the table. Would you like to eat?"

But then he says, "Yes, I'm very hungry, but unfortunately, I need to make a phone call first. Could you hold the supper just a little while until I'm done with my phone call?"

What is your response going to be? Would you say to the Lord, "Now, wait a minute. The supper's on the table already. Eat now and make your phone call later." No. Not one of you would say that to Jesus.

You would say "That's fine, Lord. I'll put it back in the oven and keep it warm. You make Your phone call, and then I'll put it on the table when you are ready. Anything you want, Lord."

Beloved sisters, this is the picture of what God is saying in Ephesians 5:22. When you take that verse and look at it in light of all those definitions of reverence, you can see this is how God is telling you to relate to your husband.

Is he worthy of that kind of treatment? No. But Jesus is, and you are reverencing your husband **"as unto the Lord."** Jesus is worthy, bless his name.

Mr. and Mrs. John & Lloys Rice

I knew John Rice when he was a very old man. He was an evangelist, author, editor, preacher, and pastor. He was also well known as a family man. He and his wife raised six daughters.

As I evaluated John Rice's life recently in light of the principles I've been teaching, I came to the conclusion that maybe he should have focused more on his family. He was gone from home a lot, on the road preaching. But then I see the wide ministry he accomplished, many saved, and much work for God done. In reading about the lives of missionaries who have made huge advances in the work of evangelism, it is clear that many of these men were warriors on the front lines of a  spiritual battle. Usually war—spiritual or physical—is no place for wives or children. John Rice and his wife seem to be a family called to make this sacrifice.

Sometimes he was gone for a month before he came back to his wife and six lovely daughters. The great marvel is the fact that his daughters grew up not feeling rejected or neglected by their father. They grew into fine, lovely, godly women who married godly men who also ministered. Do you know why?

Mrs. Rice didn't spend her days whining about being left behind and having to care for the family. Instead she reverenced her husband. She would get down on her knees every day while Daddy was away and pray with those six little girls. She prayed with fervency and sincerity, "We thank you, oh God, for our daddy who is out winning souls for Christ. We thank you that he is on the front lines of the battle for you. We pray that you will bless our daddy and use him tonight while he's preaching. We pray that you will bring him home safely to us, Lord. We long for the day when he'll come home again."

When John Rice came through the door, his wife had been such a fine mother to those six little girls that they hit him with all the joy and enthusiasm they could. He wrote many books and pamphlets on marriage, and I would suspect that his wife helped him with them. He spoke of her as being his beacon, his right hand, and a wonderful mother.

Some might think he should have been home more often, but you would never know it by the way those six girls turned out. Mama reverenced her husband.

I love stories like this, especially when I have known the person and seen the family firsthand.

Chapter Eight

What is the Basis of
Honor?

**If honor were based on performance,
not one of us would get any honor.**

Let's pose a question: is honor based
on worth? Do we honor someone who is
worthy of honor? No, I believe the Bible
teaches that honor is based on position.

1 Peter 2:17 Honour all men. Love the
brotherhood. Fear God. Honour the king.

ay you are driving somewhere, going to a meeting, and all of a sudden you see those flashing blue lights in your rearview mirror. You realize a policeman is pulling you over. It doesn't matter if that cop was drunk and beating his wife the night before. You honor him because of his position. You fear him because of his power to throw you in jail.

When he gets out of his car wearing that uniform, you are going to roll down your window and say, "Yes, Officer?"

Some of you here are going to need to take on this kind of perspective in your home. You've been turning around and around this idea of reverencing and honoring your husband. Your mind is rejecting the idea of your husband being honorable. You could probably tell us how terrible he really is.

If honor were based on performance, not one of us would get any honor. But God has designed the family unit to function with honor being given to the head of the family by the wife. The children are told to honor their father and their mother. We must learn to give honor where the role or the position calls for it, not necessarily where it is deserved.

It is this system of honor that allows a regular guy to be a policeman and keep law and order in the land. If everyone knew that cop as well as his wife did, they might all roll up their windows and say, "I'm not going to do what that guy says. He's a drunk." But if everyone took on the perspective that honor should only be given to the deserving, within hours we'd have chaos and anarchy. We would beg for the principle of honor by position to be reinstated so that we could have peace again.

How is the lack of honor affecting the precious little ones in your home? The home is the first line of defense against the REAL enemy of the soul. It is all the more important that honor be reinstated there first. God help us and guide us to see his will clearly.

Sin Is Catchy

I live in Lancaster County, and around here people know genealogies pretty well. It is Amish country so there is a long line of history in every family. Many folks can tell you, "I remember Bob and his mom and dad. I remember his granddad and his granddad's granddad. I've heard stories about his great, great granddad." People around Lancaster know each other's histories, both the bad and the good.

One story that people know is about a nagging woman who continually dishonored her husband. She was always telling him how dumb he was and how he couldn't do anything right. She told him that he was a bum and nagged him because he wouldn't take on the responsibilities she thought he ought to be taking.

The nagging woman had little girls. The little girls had wide-open hearts and minds like all children do. They lived in this home where the nagging woman degraded her husband day after day.

Eventually the little girls grew up and became teenagers. All of a sudden their sweet daddy whom they had loved when they were children was wrong. He was dumb and lazy. They began to complain about their daddy and agree with their mom. When the nagging woman started picking on the dad, the girls joined in to beat him down and tell him what a bad job he was doing and how worthless he was.

The oldest daughter grew up and wanted to get married. A young man came along. He was foolish and lacking discernment, but not a bad fellow. All he could see was that this young lady was really pretty and the dress she wore was very becoming. He courted her and they married.

After they were married, you can guess what happened. The pretty girl he married began to tell him how dumb he was. She reminded him daily how everything he tried to do was worthless

That story has gone on for generations... would someone please stop it?

and wrong. She let him know all the time that he never carried his responsibilities. The whole community heard her complaints.

The young man was slowly beaten down and was made into the same image as her father. It was no surprise to anyone that within the year she found herself married to the same kind of guy her dad was. She would hiss out at him, "You are just like my dad." And he was.

On and on the story goes; on and on the family goes…

Soon babies came along. There were little girls in the house, listening to their mother telling their dad how worthless he was. They stored the cruel words in their hearts and watched their father cringe away from their mother. In only a few years they grew up to join her merciless slander against him. Daddy was dumb and worthless. He could never pay the bills on time. He could never do anything right.

On and on the story goes; on and on the family goes… trodden down and without hope. It's a sad story and everyone knows it and thinks it is sad but entertaining. That story has gone on for generations in more than just one family. Would someone please stop it?

Would you, dear sister, stop that story in your life? Your great grandmother, your grandmother, your mother, and now you are causing destruction in the home. But you can break it. The power is in your hands to build your house instead of tearing it down.

If you are a young lady and this poison is in you, don't get married. For the sake of the children and the children's children, just don't get married. The only other harmless option is to repent toward God and change so completely that you break the cycle for good.

If you have a daughter like this, please, for pity's sake, let the young man know when he comes courting. It wouldn't be right to not warn a fellow about the misery he's about to experience and perpetuate. Have some mercy and tell him, "She may be pretty, but wait until you cross her. She has a way of picking a little here and a little there. She will make you wish you could just crawl away and hide. She will destroy your family."

Proverbs 14:1 Every wise woman buildeth her house: but the foolish plucketh it down with her hands.

Proverbs 31:26 She openeth her mouth with wisdom; and in her tongue is the law of kindness.

Proverbs 21:9 It is better to dwell in a corner of the housetop, than with a brawling woman in a wide house.

Proverbs 27:15 A continual dropping in a very rainy day and a contentious woman are alike.

Chapter Nine

A Challenging Question

God is looking for help meets, ladies who will honor what he said in his "letter of instructions,"

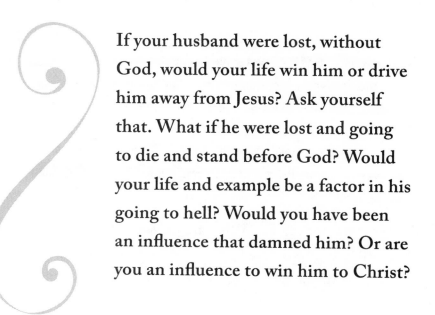

If your husband were lost, without God, would your life win him or drive him away from Jesus? Ask yourself that. What if he were lost and going to die and stand before God? Would your life and example be a factor in his going to hell? Would you have been an influence that damned him? Or are you an influence to win him to Christ?

In Closing

*D*oes your husband have problems? Yes, as a son of Adam I am sure he does. Are there needs in his life? No doubt. What can you do about it?

God spoke through the prophet Jeremiah who was living in a time when there was extreme trouble everywhere. The men of Israel were so much worse than anything you could probably imagine. They truly had turned away from their responsibilities and turned away from the God of their fathers and his law. They had turned away from all that he had instructed them to do. God describes them as a nation of liars and deceivers. Great judgment was coming, so God called to the women.

God spoke to the women of the land through Jeremiah the prophet, saying,

> **Jeremiah 9:17–18 Thus saith the LORD of hosts, Consider ye, and call for the mourning women, that they may come; and send for cunning women, that they may come:**
>
> **And let them make haste, and take up a wailing for us, that our eyes may run down with tears, and our eyelids gush out with waters.**

What are they praying for? What are they wailing and crying for? "God, would you break the hearts of our men until their eyes gush with tears?" That is the prayer the prophet called the women to pray.

Jeremiah 9:19–20 For a voice of wailing is heard out of Zion, How are we spoiled! we are greatly confounded, because we have forsaken the land, because our dwellings have cast us out.

Yet hear the word of the LORD, O ye women, and let your ear receive the word of his mouth, and teach your daughters wailing, and every one her neighbor lamentation.

God tells us through the prophet Jeremiah what you, our ladies, are supposed to do when everything is falling apart. God says, "Pray."

God doesn't say, "Rise up and take the lead and tell your husband what he ought to be doing."

God doesn't say, "Rise up and take control of the home and make the problems go away."

God told them through Jeremiah to rise up and cry out in the night and weep before God. Take up a wailing. Instead of criticizing your husband, get your daughters on their knees beside you and take up a wailing for your husband, for the men who have fallen and don't know what they are doing. Weep and pray for the

While you weep and pray for your husband, remember to reverence, honor, believe, encourage, and love him.

men who have lost their way because of the mixed-up, confused world they grew up in.

I encourage you, my sisters, to take this path. While you weep and pray for your husband, remember to reverence, honor, believe, encourage, and love him. He may not be perfect when all this is done. He may not be perfect ten years from now. He may never be all that you dream and wish he would be. But I guarantee you that he'll be a lot further down the road of right-doing than he is now.

I believe you are listening to the Spirit of God and receiving from him. Cry out to God and let him cleanse you of what is past. You will do much better in the future if you do so. Purge your conscience and let God make you free of guilt. Let him purify your heart and strengthen you to go forward and deal with these issues. His strength is sufficient for you. His strength is made perfect in weakness. Bless the name of Jesus. Amen.

God is awesome and terrible in his judgments. He is also full of mercy,

and of grace. His strong desire is to bless his people, but too often by our "carelessness," we force him to judge. I believe he wearies of judgment.

He is looking, searching, calling out to those who will hear him. He calls your name, just as long ago in the night hours he called the boy, Samuel. Just as he came to the handmaiden, Mary, he softly calls your name. Will you hear him?

God is looking for *help meets*, ladies who will honor what he said in his "letter of instructions," so he can use them as vessels of blessings. Blessings! He has so many blessings and so few willing vessels.

I can almost see him standing there, leaning over the portals of Heaven, watching, waiting, and listening for that lovely musical sound of joyful laughter wafting up through the heavens. "Yes, I hear one answering the call. Bring me the cup." An angel hands over the cup of chastisement and judgment, and God replies, "No, not THAT one; the large one full of blessings is what this little gal needs." And the angel smiles as he puts the large Blessings Cup into God's eager hands. Smiling, God begins to pour the blessings forth, spilling out blessings faster than they can be received. The angel leans over so he can see, and then he, too, hears the beautiful sound of thanksgiving floating ever upward as a sweet aroma to God. He is an Awesome God of blessings and delight. He is ever willing and ready to bless those who honor him.

Do you hear him? He is softly and tenderly calling your name: "Be the *help meet* I created you to be. Believe me, trust me, obey me, and then watch what I will do."

Showers of blessings!
Oh, that today they might fall.

For your reading pleasure, please enjoy the following chapters from Debi Pearl's bestselling book,

CREATED
TO BE HIS
Help Meet

Chapter 8

Wisdom to Understand Your Man

Co-authored by Rebekah (Pearl) Anast

A wise woman learns to adapt to her husband.

Three Kinds of Men

Men are not all the same. I have become aware that there are basically three types of men. The different types are just as marked in one-year-olds as they are in adult men. It seems that God made each male to express one side of his triad nature. No single man completely expresses the well-rounded image of God. If a man were all three types at the same time, he would be the perfect man, but I have never met, heard of, or read in a book of history or fiction of a man who is the proper balance of all three. Certainly Jesus was the perfect balance. Most men are a little of all three, but tend to be dominant in one. And all the training and experiences of life will never successfully make a man into a different type of man. There is nothing clumsier and more pathetic than a man trying to act differently from who he is. As we review the types, you will probably readily identify your husband and be able to see where you have been a curse or a blessing to him.

By the time a young woman gets married, she has developed a composite image of what her husband ought to be like. The men she has known and the characters in books and movies provide each woman with a concept of the perfect man. Poor guys! Our preconceived ideas make it tough on them. They are never perfect—far from it. God gave each one a nature that in part is like himself, but never complete. When you add in the factor that all men are fallen creatures, it makes a girl wonder why she would ever want to tie her life to one of these sons of Adam. But God made us ladies to have this unreasonable desire to be needed by a man, and our hormones are working strenuously to bring us together.

> *If you fight his inadequacies, both of you will fail. If you love him and support him <u>with</u> his inadequacies and <u>without</u> taking charge, both of you will succeed and grow.*

When a girl suddenly finds herself permanently wed to a man who is not like she thinks he ought to be, rather than adapt to him, she usually spends the rest of their marriage—which may not be very long—trying to change him into what she thinks her man ought to be. Most young girls are married only a short time when they make the awful discovery that they may have gotten a lemon. Rather than bemoan your "fate," ask God for wisdom.

Wisdom is knowing what you "bought" when you married that man, and learning to adapt to him *as he is*, not as you want him to be.

Men are not alike. Your husband most likely will not be like your father or brother or the man in your favorite romance novel. Our husbands are created in the image of God, and it takes all kinds of men to even come close to completing that image. No man is a perfect balance; if he were, he would be too divine to need you. **God gives imperfect women to imperfect men so they can be heirs together of the grace of life and *become something more together than either one of them would ever be alone.*** If you fight your husband's inadequacies or seek to be dominant where he is not, both of you will fail. If you love him and support him <u>with</u> his inadequacies and <u>without</u> taking charge, both of you will succeed and grow.

Mr. Command Man

God is **dominant**—a sovereign and all-powerful God. He is also **visionary**—omniscient and desirous of carrying out his plans. And, God is **steady**—the same yesterday, and today, and forever, our faithful High Priest. Most men epitomize one of these three aspects of God.

A few men are born with more than their share of dominance and, on the surface, a deficit in gentleness. They often end up in positions that command other men. We will call them *Command Men*. They are born leaders. They are often chosen by other men to be military commanders, politicians, preachers and heads of corporations. Winston Churchill, George Patton, and Ronald Reagan are examples of dominant men. Since our world needs only a few leaders, God seems to limit the number of these *Command Men*. Throughout history, men created in God the Father's image have all surrounded themselves with good men to help get big jobs completed. *Command Men* usually do more than is required of them.

They are known for expecting their wives to wait on them hand and foot. A *Command Man* does not want his wife involved in any project that prevents her from serving him. If you are blessed to be married to a strong, forceful, bossy man, as I am, then it is very important for you to learn how to make an appeal without challenging his authority. We will discuss how to make an appeal later in this book.

> It is very important for you to learn how to make an appeal without challenging his authority.

Command Men have less tolerance, so they will often walk off and leave their clamoring wife before she has a chance to realize that she is even close to losing her marriage. By the time she realizes that there is a serious problem, she is already a divorced mother seeking help in how to raise her children alone. A woman can fight until she is blue in the face, yet the *Command Man* will not yield. He is not as intimate or vulnerable as are other men in sharing his personal feelings or vocation with his wife. **He seems to be sufficient unto himself.** It is awful being shut out. A woman married to a *Command Man* has to **earn her place in his heart** by proving that she will stand by her man, faithful, loyal, and obedient. When she has won his confidence, he will treasure her to the extreme.

She is on call every minute of her day. Her man wants to know where she is, what she is doing, and why she is doing it. He corrects her without thought. For better or for worse, it is his nature to control.

A woman married to a *Command Man* wears a heavier yoke than most women, but it can be a very rewarding yoke. In a way, her walk as his help meet is easier because there is never any possibility of her being in control. There are no gray areas; she always knows exactly what is required of her, therefore she has a calm sense of safety and rest.

The *Command Man* feels it his duty and responsibility to lead people, and so he does, whether they think they want him to lead or not. Amazingly, this is what the public is most comfortable with. Very few people have enough confidence to strike out on their own; plus, the feeling of being blamed for mistakes holds them back. The *Command Man* is willing to take the chance, and for that purpose God created these king-like men. Their road is not easy, for James said, **"My brethren, be not many masters, knowing that we shall receive the greater condemnation"** (James 3:1).

On 9-11, when the World Trade Center was destroyed, another plane flying over Pennsylvania was being highjacked by other terrorists. Mr. Todd Beamer was on that plane. It was his voice we all heard saying the now famous line, "Let's roll."

He must have been a strong *Mr. Command Man*. He, and others like him, took control of a desperate situation and saved many other lives while sacrificing their own. It could have been a terrible mistake, but Mr. Beamer evaluated the situation, made a decision, and then acted upon it. He knew the lives of all those people were in his hands. It was a heavy responsibility, yet he was "willing to do what a man's gotta do." You will remember how strong and queenly his young widow seemed when we watched her on TV after the attacks. **A good *Mr. Command* sees the bigger picture and strives to help the greatest number,** even if it costs him his life and the lives of those he loves. If he is an honest man, he will take financial loss in order to help lead those who need him, but in the end he will usually come out on top. If he is not an honest man, he will be selfish and use the resources of others to further his own interests.

> A King wants a Queen, which is why a man in command wants a faithful wife to share his fame and glory.

A King wants a Queen, which is why a man in command wants a faithful wife to share his fame and glory. Without a woman's admiration, his victories are muted. **If a wife learns early to enjoy the benefits of taking the second seat, and if she does not take offense to his headstrong aggressiveness, she will be the one sitting at his right side being adored, because this kind**

A King needs a Queen with whom to share his glory

of man will totally adore his woman and exalt her. She will be his closest, and sometimes his only, confidante. Over the years, the *Command Man* can become more yielding and gentle. His wife will discover secret portals to his heart.

If you are married to a king, honor and reverence is something you must give him on a daily basis if you want him to be a benevolent, honest, strong, and fulfilled man of God. He has the potential to become an amazing leader. Never shame him, and do not belittle him or ignore his accomplishments.

If the wife of a *Command Man* resists his control, he will readily move forward without her. If he is not a principled Christian, he will allow the marriage to come to divorce. Like King Ahasuerus of Persia, if she defies him, he will replace her and not look back. If his Christian convictions prevent him from divorcing, he will remain stubbornly in command, and she will be known as a miserable old wretch.

> His vision is like a man looking from a mountaintop; he sees the distant goal.

If a *Command Man* has not developed working skills, and thus accomplishes little, he will have the tendency to tell stories about himself and brag until people are sick of him. If he has left his wife and lost his children, thus having no legitimate "kingdom" of his own, he will be obnoxiously garrulous.

A *Command Man* who has gone bad is likely to be abusive. It is important to remember that much of how a *Command Man* reacts depends on his wife's reverence toward him. **When a *Command Man* (lost or saved) is treated with honor and reverence, a good help meet will find that her man will be wonderfully protective and supportive.** In most marriages, the strife is not because the man is cruel or evil; it is because he expects obedience, honor, and reverence, and is not getting it. Thus, he reacts badly. When a wife plays her part as a help meet, the *Command Man* will respond differently. Of course, there are a few men who are so cruel and violent that even when the wife *is* a proper help meet, he will still physically abuse her or the children. In such cases, it would be the duty of the wife to alert the authorities so that they might become the arm of the Lord to do justice.

- *Mr. Command* will not take the trash out, as a general rule, and he will not clean up the mess at the trash area. He may organize and command someone else to do it. Any woman trying to force *Mr. Command* into becoming a nice trash man will likely end up alone, trashed by her man.

Chapter 8 ~ Wisdom to Understand Your Man

- *Mr. Command* will want to talk about his plans, ideas, and finished projects. He will be very objective, very unemotional, and **he will not enjoy small talk. His vision is like a man looking from a high mountain; he sees the distant goal.** He will expect his wife to help him remember individuals' needs.
- *Mr. Command Man* will be most uncomfortable and at a loss when dealing with the sick, helpless, and dying. Where there is no hope, there will be no need for a *Command Man*.
- A born leader is a man who can, when necessary, adapt principles or rules to circumstances for the greater good of the greatest number of people.

Mr. Visionary

God is a *Visionary* as seen in his person, the Holy Spirit. He made some men in the image of that part of his nature. Prophets, be they true or false, are usually of this type. Some of you are married to men who are shakers, changers, and dreamers. These men get the entire family upset about peripheral issues, such as: do we believe in Christmas? Should we use state marriage licenses? Should a Christian opt out of the Social Security system? The issues may be serious and worthy of one's commitment, but, in varying degrees, these men have tunnel vision, tenaciously focusing on single issues. They will easily pick up and relocate without any idea of what they are going to do for a living at their new location. They are often the church splitters and the ones who demand doctrinal purity and proper dress and conduct. Like a prophet, they call people to task for their inconsistencies. If they are not wise, they can be real fools who push their agendas, forcing others to go their way. One *Visionary* will campaign for the legalization of pot, while another will be an activist to make abortions illegal. Most will just sit around the house and complain, but in their souls they are *Visionaries*.

> Learn how to be flexible, and learn how to always be loyal to your man.

Visionaries are often gifted men or inventors, and I am sure it was men of this caliber who conquered the Wild West, though they would not have been the farmers who settled it. Today, *Visionary* men are street preachers, political activists, organizers and instigators of any front-line social issue. **They love confrontation**, and hate the status quo. "Why leave it the way it is when you can change it?" They are the

A Visionary needs a stable, wise wife 🖤

men who keep the rest of the world from getting stagnant or dull. **The *Visionary* is consumed with a need to communicate with his words, music, writing, voice, art, or actions.** He is the "**voice crying out in the wilderness**" striving to change the way humanity is behaving or thinking. Good intentions don't always keep *Visionaries* from causing great harm. They can stir up pudding and end up with toxic waste, if they are not wise. An unwise wife can add to the poison with negative words, or she can, with simple words of caution, bring attention to the goodness of the pudding and the wisdom in leaving it alone. **Every *Mr. Visionary* needs a good, wise, prudent, stable wife who has a positive outlook on life.**

If you are married to one of these fellows, expect to be rich or poor, rarely middle class. He may invest everything in a chance and lose it all or make a fortune, but he will not do well working 8 to 5 in the same place for thirty years, and then retiring to live the good life. If he works a regular job, he may either not show up half the time or he will work like a maniac 80 hours a week and love every minute. He may purchase an alligator farm in Florida or a ski resort in Colorado, or he may buy an old house trailer for $150 with hopes of fixing it up and selling it for $10,000, only to find out that it is so deteriorated that it can't be moved. He will then have his wife and all the kids help him tear the top off and carry the scraps to the dump, (saving the appliances in the already crowded garage), so he can make a farm trailer out of the axles. Now that he has a farm trailer and no animals, expect him to get a deal on three, old, sick cows, and… **He may never be rich in money, but he will be rich in experience.**

Greatness is a state of soul, not certain accomplishments.

Come to think of it, maybe my husband is not a 100% *Mr. Command Man*, because he seems quite a bit like this *Mr. Visionary*. I remember, on more than one occasion, helping him tear down someone's old barn in order to drag the junk home to fill up our old barn. <u>Remember, most men are a mixture of types, but usually stronger in one.</u>

The wife of *Mr. Visionary* should be just a little bit reckless and blind in one eye if she is going to enjoy the ride. If this is your man, you need to learn two very important things (beyond how to make an appeal). **Learn how to be flexible, and learn how to always be loyal to your man.** You will be amazed at how much happier you will be and how much fun life can be if you learn to just go with the flow—*his flow*. Life will become an adventure. You will actually begin to feel sorry for the gals married to the stick-in-the-mud, *steady type*. And once you get it into your head that your husband does not have to be "right" for you to follow him, you will FINALLY be able to say "bye-bye" to your overwrought parents, even when they are screaming that you are married to a crazy man. People looking on will marvel that you are able to love and appreciate your husband, but you will know better because **you will see his greatness.**

Greatness is a state of soul, not certain accomplishments. Thomas Edison, though not recognized as such, was *great* after his 999th failure to make a light bulb. The Wright brothers were *great* when they neglected their lucrative occupation of fixing bicycles and "wasted time" trying to make one of them fly. If the light bulb had never worked and the plane had never flown, and no one remembered their names today, they would have been the same men, and their lives would have still been just as full and their days just as challenging. Did Edison's wife think him great when he used his last dime on another failed idea? If she didn't, just think what she missed.

> It will be your face he looks into to see the marvel of what a great thing he has done.

The *Visionary* man needs his woman's support, and he will appreciate it when it is freely given. Without her, he feels alone. This guy will be a little hard to live with at first. Big, wild fights are the usual beginnings if a nice, normal girl (who had a *Mr. Steady* daddy) marries one of "the weird ones." They will either have a bitter divorce (she divorces him) in the first few years, or she will decide to learn to appreciate him, because he is really rather lovable. I get very few letters from wives married to these high-strung, going-to-reinvent-the-wheel men. I do get lots of letters from their mothers-in-law, asking us to write and straighten out their sons-in-law.

Some of these guys talk with glowing enthusiasm and animation. Usually, they enjoy hashing over ideas, plans and dreams. If you are married to one, he loves to tell you about his newest idea, and he wants your enthusiastic support, not a critique of his idea. He will look at his idea more critically later, but for the moment, the idea itself is invigorating to him. He will have a thousand ideas for every project he attempts, and he will try many that he will never finish, and he will finish some that are worthless, and you "knew it all along." Remind him of that the next time he has an idea, and you will destroy your marriage—but you won't change him. He will share his "dumb ideas" with someone else.

Learn to Enjoy the Trip

Several years back, a newlywed couple decided to take a bicycle road trip for their honeymoon. They had the map all worked out and the bikes and camping gear ready. After riding for a couple days, the young wife noticed that her good husband was going the wrong way. She stopped him and tried to show him on the map that he had veered off the course. She had always been endowed with a natural ability to read maps and knew exactly where they were. He was not so gifted and argued that she was dead wrong and insisted that they were headed the right way. Later that day, when he did discover that he had indeed taken the wrong road, he brushed it off and blamed the signs or gave some plausible reason. Again he took the wrong road, and she argued with him. He kept correcting

> He spends his life looking through a telescope or microscope, and he will be stunned that what he sees, others do not seem to notice or care about.

their course, but they were not getting anywhere by its shortest route. She let him know his error. That part of the honeymoon was not very "honeyed." Nothing would change his mind. He knew he was right, and if not exactly right, then he was as right as could be expected under the circumstances, and criticism was not welcomed.

What could she do? The young wife was not pleased with the way they were relating, and she reasoned to herself that this could become the pattern for the rest of their lives. As she brooded on the matter, it occurred to her that it was very important to him to be right and to be in charge, and it really didn't matter which road they took. They were taking this trip to be together, not to get somewhere in particular. God in his mercy and grace gave this sweet young wife a new heart. She decided to follow her husband down any road he chose, without question or second-guessing. So she cheerfully began to enjoy the beautiful day and the glory of being young and in love as she continued to pedal her bike down a road that was taking them to where every marriage ought to go, even though it was not according to the map.

This little lady is married to a 100% *Visionary Man*. She started her marriage right, following him wherever he led, regardless of whether she thought it was the right direction or not. She has been flexible and is enjoying her ride. Someday, when her husband is assured that he can trust her with his heart, he will let her be his navigator—and still take the credit for it. The moral to this story is: the way you think

Learn to appreciate his greatness ♥

determines how you will feel, and how you feel influences the way you will act.

If you are married to the *Visionary Man*, **learn to enjoy the trip,** for if he ever does make a better light bulb, he will want you to be the one who turns it on for the first time in public. It will be your face he looks into to see the marvel of what a great thing he has done. You are his most important fan. When you know your man really needs you, you can be happy with just about anything.

Overtime, this type of man will become more practical. If you are a young wife married to a man whom your mama thinks is totally crazy—then you may be married to *Mr. Visionary*. Right now, purpose in your heart to be loyal to him, and to **be flexible**; then, let your dreamer dream. Lean back and enjoy the ride; it should prove interesting.

> The moral to this story is: the way you think determines how you will feel, and how you feel influences the way you will act.

The world needs the *Visionary Man*, for he is the one who seeks out hypocrisy and injustice and slays the dragons. He calls himself and those around him to a higher standard. He knows how to do nearly everything and is readily willing to advise others. In time, he will be quite accomplished in more than one thing.

• *Visionary Man* will take the trash out if he remembers it. But, he may also end up inventing a way whereby the trash takes itself out or is turned into an energy source, or he may just waste a lot of time building a cart for you to take it out. He will not mind cleaning up if he notices it needs doing, but he may get so deeply involved that he decides to paint while he is sweeping, and then switch projects before he gets finished painting. And he will likely be irritated when his wife nags him about it.

• *Visionary Man* will talk and talk and talk to his honey if she approves of him. He will be subjective, thinking about feelings, moods, and spiritual insights. **One of his greatest needs will be for his wife to think objectively (proven truth) and use common sense,** which will help keep his feet from flying too far from solid ground. **He spends his life looking through a telescope or microscope,** and he will be stunned that what he sees (or thinks he sees), others do not seem to notice or care about. Every small issue will become mind-consuming, and he will need his wife to casually talk about the big picture and the possible end results of relationships, finances, or health if he continues to totally focus on his present interest. His sweetheart needs to stay in a positive state of mind, yet never jump into his make-believe world, trying to be too much of a cheerleader on dead-end issues. Let him burn out on things that are not wise. But don't throw water on his fire. Let him find his own balance through bumping into hard realities. The Old Testament prophets of God must surely have been the Visionary types. Remember Elijah, Jeremiah, and Ezekiel and all their trials?

- *Visionary Man* is an initiator and provoker. He is a point man, trailblazer, and a voice to get things done. He will start and keep the party going until the *Command Man* gets there to lead on.

- **Visionary Man's focus is so intense that matters can easily be blown out of proportion.** A wife must guard against negative conversation about people. An idle conversation by her can bring about the end of a life-long friendship. This is true with all men, but especially so with *Mr. Visionary*. Search your heart and discover your motive in what you say about people. What is your intent when you speak? To build him up and give him joy, or to build up yourself and make him think that you alone are perfect? If you mention people and make them look a little bad and yourself a little "taken for granted," your husband may get the idea that friends and family are treating you unfairly, and he may become withdrawn and suspicious. You could unwittingly render your husband unteach-

> One of his greatest needs will be for his wife to think objectively and use common sense.

able. If you want your husband to grow into a confident, outgoing man of God, then he needs to have a clear conscience toward his friends and family. God says a woman's conversation can win her lost husband. In the same vein, a woman's idle, negative conversation can cripple a strong man and cause him to become an angry, confrontational, divisive man. **"Likewise, ye wives, be in subjection to your own husbands; that, if any obey not the word, they also may without the word <u>be won by the conversation of the wives</u>; While they behold your <u>chaste conversation</u> coupled with fear"** (1 Peter 3:1-2).

- *Mr. Visionary* needs a lady who does not take offense easily. She needs to be tough. He needs his lady to be full of life and joy. A *Visionary Man* is not equipped to be a comforter—for himself or anyone else. His lady will need to learn to tuck in that quivering lip, square those shoulders, and put on that smile.

- *Mr. Visionary* can be a leader, but because he has tunnel vision his leadership will have a more narrow focus.

♥ Learning to be his help meet ♥

115

Mr. Steady

God is as steady as an eternal rock, caring, providing, and faithful, like a priest—*like Jesus Christ*. He created many men in that image. We will call him *Mr. Steady*—"in the middle, not given to extremes." The *Steady Man* does not make snap decisions or spend his last dime on a new idea, and he doesn't try to tell other people what to do. He avoids controversy. He doesn't invent the light bulb like *Mr. Visionary*, but he will be the one to build the factory and manage the assembly line that produces the light bulb and the airplane. He does not jump to the front of the plane to take a razor knife away from a terrorist, unless he is encouraged to do so by *Mr. Command*. He would never lead a revolution against the government or the church. He will quietly ignore hypocrisy in others. He will selflessly fight the wars that *Mr. Visionary* starts and *Mr. Command* leads. He builds the oil tankers, farms the soil, and quietly raises his family. As a general rule, he will be faithful till the day he dies in the same bed he has slept in for the last 40 or 50 years. Older women who are divorced and have learned by their mistakes **know the value of peace and safety, and they will long for a nice steady man of his stature, but such a man is rarely available**—unless his foolish wife has left him. This man is content with the wife of his youth.

> Your husband's gentleness is not a weakness; it is his strength. Your husband's hesitation is not indecision; it is cautious wisdom.

Joys and Tribulations

Being married to a *Steady Man* has its rewards and its trials. On the good side, your husband never puts undue pressure on you to perform miracles. He doesn't expect you to be his servant. You do not spend your days putting out emotional fires, because he doesn't create tension in the family. You rarely feel hurried, pushed, pressured, or forced. The women married to *Visionary Men* look at you in wonder that your husband seems so balanced and stable. The wife of *Command Man* marvels at the free time you seem to have. If your dad happened to be a *Steady Man*, then chances are you will appreciate your husband's down-to-earth, practical life for the wonderful treasure it is.

When you are married to a man who is steady and cautious, and you have a bit of the impatient romantic in you, you may not see his worth and readily honor him. You may be discontent because he is slow and cautious to take authority or make quick decisions. A bossy woman sees her husband's lack of hasty judgment and calls her *Steady* husband "wishy-washy." His steadiness makes him the last to change, so he seems to be a follower because he is seldom out front forming up the troops. There is no exciting rush in him, just a slow, steady climb with no bells or whistles. You wish he would just make up his mind, and that he would take a stand in the church. He seems to just let people use him. There are times you wish he would boldly tell you what to do so you would not have to carry all the burden of decision-making.

Some women equate their husband's wise caution and lack of open passion as being unspiritual. His lack of spontaneity and open boldness may look like indifference to spiritual things. However, he is like deep, deep water. The very depth makes the movement almost imperceptible, but it is, nevertheless, very strong.

He will be confused with your unhappiness and try to serve you more, which may further diminish your respect for his masculinity. **Disappointment and unthankfulness can make you wearier than any amount of duties.** The trials he seems to cause you are really your discontented responses to what you consider to be his shortcomings. If you didn't attempt to change him into something other than what God created him to be, he would not cause you any grief. His very steadiness keeps him on his middle-of-the-road course, and it will drive a controlling woman crazy.

This is why many disgruntled ladies married to Mr. Steadys fall victim to hormonal imbalance, physical illness, or emotional problems.

When a woman is married to a bossy, dominant man, people marvel that she is willing to serve him without complaint, so she comes out looking like a wonderful woman of great patience and sacrifice. A woman married to the impulsive *Visionary Man,* who puts the family through hardships, will stir amazement in everyone. "How can she tolerate his weird ideas with such peace and joy?" She comes out being a real saint, maybe even a martyr. But if you are married to a wonderful, kind, loving, serving man, and you are just a little bit selfish, then you are likely to end up looking like an unthankful shrew. He helps you, adores you, protects you, and is careful to provide for you, and you are still not satisfied. Shame on you!

The Foot Washer

Yesterday, I used a water hose to wash the inside of the church outhouse. For you city girls, an outhouse is a small hut sitting over a hole in the ground, with a

Mr. Steady is the most social of the three types 🖤

wooden floor, and a seat with a hole in it. Before indoor plumbing, this was a typical toilet. The outhouse usually sat about 50 feet from the house. As you can imagine, outhouses stink. As I squirted water over the walls and potty, I was wishing Chuck was around. If there is a dirty job, a tiresome job, a job which most people will try to avoid, a job where there is no glory to be found, you can be sure that Chuck will be there, quietly taking responsibility.

Our friend Chuck is a "foot-washer." His strength is best seen in what he does for others. When I read the story of Jesus washing the animal manure off of the disciples' feet, or calling the little children to come unto him, or feeding the five thousand, I think of Chuck. The disciples all wanted to be in charge, to be seen, to receive glory. But Christ spent most of his time with them teaching them to be quiet servants—the works of a Steady Man.

Jesus was a foot-washer. In Christ's time, washing the feet of the traveler was a loathsome job that befell the lowest paid servant, yet Jesus washed their feet as a testimony to them of what he values. **"If I then, your Lord and Master, have washed your feet; ye also ought to wash one another's feet"** (John 13:12). In effect, he was teaching them, "If you want to be my disciple, then plan on spending your life cleaning up after folks, fixing the old lady's sink, and driving out of your way to give someone a ride to the church."

Many women think of their pastor as a mighty man of God, or their song leader as a spirit-filled man. Yet, I suspect it will be the quiet Mr. Steady-type men who will be called the "greatest in the kingdom of Heaven." The Steady Man, the quiet man, the man who does not take control, is not a man of little worth, for Jesus exalted the common chores that are so often performed by the Steady Man. Mr. Steady can be a strong man of God. His strength is exercised as he quietly assumes responsibility that others usually shirk. If we as wives could only learn to honor the man God gave us, we would be blessed to see what a mighty man of God he could become. A glorious marriage is sometimes only an appreciation away. Ask God for wisdom to honor and appreciate your Steady Man.

"Even as the Son of man came not to be ministered unto, but to minister, and to give his life a ransom for many" (Matthew 20:28).

"And there was also a strife among them, which of them should be accounted the greatest. And he said unto them, The kings of the Gentiles exercise lordship over them; and they that exercise author-

Chapter 8 - Wisdom to Understand Your Man

ity upon them are called benefactors. But ye shall not be so: but he that is greatest among you, let him be as the younger; and he that is chief, as he that doth serve. For whether is greater, he that sitteth at meat, or he that serveth? is not he that sitteth at meat? but <u>I am among you as he that serveth</u>" (Luke 22:24-27).

Know Your Man

Wives are very much flesh and blood, and as young women, we don't come to marriage with all the skills needed to make it start out good, let alone perfect. When you come to know your man for whom God created him to be, you will stop trying to change him into what you *think* he should be. **The key is to know your man. If he is *Mr. Steady,* you need to learn to be thankful and to honor him as the one created for you in the image of God.** God's Word says in Hebrews 13:8, **"Jesus Christ the same yesterday, and to day, and for ever." A man who is created steady brings peace and safety to a woman's soul.** Your husband's gentleness is not a weakness; **it is his strength.** Your husband's hesitation is not indecision; it is cautious wisdom. Your husband's lack of deep spiritual conversation is not a lack of caring; it is simply the cap on a mountain of intense emotions. If he ever speaks of how he does feel, he will most likely become teary.

He wants to please you. **"Counsel in the heart of man is like deep water; but a man** [a wife also] **of understanding will draw it out"** (Proverbs 20:5). You will not need to learn how to make an appeal to him, because your husband is all too willing to hear you.

If this describes your man, you need to learn how to stand still and listen; then let God move your husband in his own good time. Ask God for wisdom and patience. Seek to always have a gentle spirit. Look up "shamefacedness" in the Bible, and learn what it means. Pray for your husband to have wisdom. Stop expecting him to *perform* for you, to pray with the family, to speak out in witnessing, or to take a bold stand at church. **Stop trying to stir him up to anger** toward the children in order to get him to feel as though he understands how badly you are being treated. **Let him be the one God made him to be: a still, quiet, thoughtful presence**—*for you!* *Command* and *Visionary Men* understand and appreciate him, and they, too, lean on this type of man for stability. Learn to seek your husband's advice on what to do, and then give him time to answer, even if it means days or weeks. Show respect by asking him in what areas he would like you to do some decision-making.

Mr. Steady likes to serve ♥

119

Many of these "nice" men prefer their wives to show some initiative. A *Command Man* tells you what to do and how to serve him, and a *Visionary Man* wants you to do what he is doing.

A *Steady Man* likes a woman to walk beside him, yet grow in her own right before God and him.

If you are married to a *Mr. Steady*, you need to get familiar with Proverbs 31 to know how to be an active help meet to your man (see page 222). Your husband will enjoy and share your triumphs in business. He will be proud of your accomplishments. He will want you to use your natural skills, abilities, and drives. Your achievements will be an honor to him, but lazy slothfulness will greatly discourage him. Your wasting of time and spending money foolishly will weigh heavily on him, robbing him of his pride and pleasure in you. **He needs a resourceful, hardworking woman with dignity and honor. It is important to *Mr. Steady* that his wife be self-sufficient in all the mundane tasks of daily living.** You must learn how to pay bills, make appointments, and entertain guests with a competence that brings him satisfaction. Your hobbies should be creative and useful, involving your children so that all of you are busy and productive every day. Your home should be clean and orderly so that his friends and business contacts will be impressed and at ease. Your skills and achievements are your husband's résumé. If you are wise and competent, then he must be even more so, the onlooker will think. At the end of the day, *Mr. Steady* will enjoy weighing what he has accomplished with what you have accomplished and will rejoice in the value of having a worthy partner in the grace of life.

These men can be some of the most important men in the church, because their steadfastness is sure, and their loyalty is strong. **They make wise, well-thought-out decisions.** They are rarely rash or foolish, although (to their discredit) they will sometimes tolerate foolishness or error without dissent. Their children grow up to highly respect their gentle-speaking dad. If mother has been negative towards Dad, the adult children will strongly resent her to the point of disliking her.

Typically, *Steady Men* do not become as well known as *Command* or *Visionary Men*. They are not odd or stand-out men. They are not loud. They are neither irritating nor particularly magnificent. If they do rise to public notice, it will be because of an enormity of achievement or because they are trusted for their very visible traits of honesty and steadiness. Women and men alike envy and desire a *Command Man*. People are often drawn and compelled by the *Visionary*. But the *Steady Man* is taken for granted. He is seldom a campaigner. He is needed, but not flashy enough to win the spotlight. He will never brag on himself and is typically very poor at "selling" himself and his skills. He waits for another to point out his value and call for his help. It is your job to "sell" him, to speak highly of him until all are convinced and aware that he is the skillful professional they've been looking for.

The vast majority of my letters are from women criticizing their laid-back, quiet, slow, unassuming, undemanding, hardworking husbands for their "carnal" habits. These wives have forgotten to have a life of their own, so they spend their time trying to remake their husbands into dominant types because they admire leadership, authority, and clout. They don't have a clue about the demands that come from being married to a dominant, bossy man.

Most of this book has been written to help young wives learn to honor, obey, and appreciate the *Steady Man* just as he is. If a wife dishonors her steady husband and takes control, he will most likely stay with her; they probably will not divorce. But her dishonor will cause him to lack the confidence to further his business opportunities. He will become satisfied with the mediocre, because it involves no risk. He will know that he pulls the plow alone, that he has no helper. Yet, if that same man had married a thankful, creative woman who delighted in him and thought he was the smartest, wisest, most important fellow around, then he would have risen to the occasion in every area of his life. Many women believe *Mr. Steady* is mediocre and lacks strength and authority, when in actuality, *Mr. Steady* is a manly, steady fellow that lacks a good wife.

- *Mr. Steady* may take the trash out and always keep the area clean, yet his wife will be prone to take his goodness for granted.

- He will be in quiet contemplation much of the time. It will drive his wife crazy, because she will long for him to share his deepest feelings and thoughts with her so she can "feel" loved. He cannot. He might even cry during times of stress or intimacy. He is very, very slow to come to trust and open up to the woman he loves, because he does not understand her. He will enjoy the company of others and be most comfortable spending time in small talk with whoever is around. **Of the three types, he is the one who will be most liked by everyone.**

- *Mr. Steady* is always in demand. People everywhere need him to fix a car, build a house, set up their computer, figure out what's wrong with their phone, heal

♥ Learn to be a help meet to the man God gave to you ♥

them of cancer, and the list goes on and on. You begin to wonder if you will ever have him all to yourself. The answer is, no. He belongs to people. When it is time or past time for some special time alone, take a vacation, and *leave the cell phone at home.*

- The *Steady Man* is wonderful with those who are hurt, sick, or dying. **He loves to comfort** and seems to know what a person needs in times of great sorrow. **His still, quiet presence brings peace.** To the *Command Man,* this is nothing short of a miracle. A *Steady Man* thrust into a *Command Man's* position or job will be stressed and, in the end, unsuccessful. He is not meant to lead, but to support.

- He does not focus on the eternal picture, nor is he looking through a microscope, but he does respect both views as important. **His vision is as a man seeing life just as it is.** He can shift his sights to the sky and know there is more up there than he can see, and he wonders about it. Or, he can stare into a muddy pond and appreciate that there is a whole world in there that he knows nothing about. In most of life, he is a bridge between the other two types of men. He is a very necessary expression of God's image.

"Ruination" Wife's Summary

a) The wife of *Mr. Command Man* can ruin her marriage by failing to honor, obey, and reverence her husband's authority and rule.

b) The wife of *Mr. Visionary* can ruin her marriage by failing to follow, believe, and participate as an enthusiast in her husband's dreams and visions.

c) The wife of *Mr. Steady* can ruin her marriage by failing to appreciate, wait on, and be thankful for her husband's pleasant qualities.

Successful Wife's Summary

a) The wife of *Mr. Command Man* can heal her marriage by becoming his adoring Queen, honoring and obeying his every (reasonable and unreasonable) word. She will dress, act, and speak so as to bring him honor everywhere she goes.

💗 Mr. Steady needs his wife to like him just as he is 💗

b) The wife of *Mr. Visionary* can heal her marriage by laying aside her own dreams and aspirations and embracing her role as help meet to her man, believing in him and being willing to follow him with joyful participation in the path he has chosen.

c) The wife of *Mr. Steady* can heal her marriage by joyfully realizing what a friend, lover, and companion she has been given and living that gratitude verbally and actively. When she stops trying to change him, he will grow. She can, then, willingly take up tasks that will fill her time and give her husband joy and satisfaction when he sees her productiveness.

TIME TO CONSIDER

Who is *your* man?

Make a list of your husband's traits—things that indicate which of the three types he most expresses. It may be a combination, with one more dominant. Now, begin a list of things you can do that will set him free to be the man God made him to be.

"I beseech you therefore, brethren, by the mercies of God, that ye present your bodies a living sacrifice, holy, acceptable unto God, which is your reasonable service. And be not conformed to this world: but <u>be ye transformed by the renewing of your mind</u>, that ye may prove what is that good, and acceptable, and <u>perfect, will of God</u>" (Romans 12:1-2).

Ask God to give you wisdom to see where you need to change to be the perfect help meet for your divinely designed man.

Keep in mind that most men
are a little of all three types,
but tend to be stronger in one.

Chapter 9

Finding Your Life in His

From the beginning, God meant for us to be a comfort, a blessing, a reward, a friend, an encouragement, and a right-hand wo-man.

Memories That Matter

I watched a movie one time called "Dad." It told the story of an old couple in their final years. The wife treated her husband as inept, controlling him and always jumping to supply his every need with a patronizing air. She wouldn't even let him pour the milk on his cereal. He seemed to be senile—living in a hazy world. The grown son came home to help the old parents in their last days. The old lady had spent her life controlling and taking care of her Mr. Nice, Steady Husband. But while the old woman was in the hospital with an ailment, the old man, at the encouragement of his middle-aged son, started going places and doing fun things. Suddenly, "Grandfather" seemed years younger. It was like the calendar was turned back fifty years. He was happy now. When Grandma got out of the hospital, she came home to a changed man. With great enthusiasm, he talked of friends and family that actually never existed. He spoke of the dairy farm and their life on it. He spoke of their four children—but they only had two. He spoke with longing of his much loved, gentle, and obedient wife—quite different from the reality he'd experienced over their many years together. His wife was terribly shaken, because she knew there never had been a dairy farm, nor were there more than two children. She knew the woman he remembered so fondly was not her.

A psychologist was called in to try to explain what was happening to the old man's mind. The doctor explained to the family that for fifty years Grandfather had worked faithfully at the same factory, doing the same old job with his hands, but while his hands worked, his mind was dreaming of the life he really wanted. It was a life of sunshine and hard work on a dairy farm with his large family of children helping him. **As Grandfather's mind aged, the pleasant, make-believe world he had lived out in his imagination became more real to him than the caged life he had actually lived.** Because of his wife's controlling hand and his desire to "do his duty" and please her, he had failed to live his dreams. She had weakened him with her control and criticism until he created an imaginary world of hope and fulfillment. This simple story illustrated so well the sad reality of many families.

The CPA

This letter came from a lady whose husband decided to make his dreams come true. It would have taken a book the size of this one to explain to her why she needs to be her husband's dream lady. I know this is what she really wants. She has just temporarily lost her vision.

> *Dear Pearls,*
>
> *I have been married for 19 years, and my husband really is a great guy. He knows the Lord, but has not been as consistent with his Bible reading as I'd like to see. I am not saying anything to him about it yet. Our problems really stem from a change he made for our family that started about three years ago.*
>
> *When we married, he was studying to be a CPA. I helped him through the last year of his schooling and spent 15 years with*

him going through long hours of tax seasons. I didn't like it much, but I knew that was his career. He wanted to find some job that would let him stay at home and be his own boss. I thought that was a noble cause, and I wanted him to be with our sons as they grew up.

Well, what he has decided to do now, I can hardly handle! He decided to become a dairy farmer. We are city people. I told him all along, I really didn't have a desire to be a dairy farmer. For three years, all he has done is read and research on it. I know he can make it work; it is just not something I want to do. I have had to cope with a lot. He still works in town and rushes home to go work in the barn. I had to wait dinner on him last night until 7 PM, and then he rushes home and goes straight to the barn. I was really hurt. I am tired of working and feeling as though we are getting nowhere. This is tearing the family apart. I know I must be submissive, but I truly do not want to do this. It is not my dream. There was no talk of farming 19 years ago!

> *Yolanda*

Yolanda's concept of marriage is all wrong, not at all like God's intention for marriage. God didn't create Adam and Eve at the same time and then tell them to work out some compromise on how they would each achieve their personal goals in a cooperative endeavor. He created Adam, gave him an occupation, appointed him as ruler of the planet, endowed him with a spiritual outlook, gave him commands, and specified his occupational duties. Adam commenced his rule of the planet **before God created Eve to help him in his life's goals.** Adam didn't need to get Eve's consent. **God gave her to Adam to be HIS helper, not his partner. She was designed to serve,** not to be served, **to assist,** not to veto his decisions. Talk about a change of occupation and habitation! Look at Eve. Can you imagine her saying something like this to Adam? *"When God brought me to you in that wonderful garden, and we commenced life together, you never said anything about thorns and thistles, about pain in childbirth, about milking goats and churning butter. I am not a wilderness girl!"*

> God made us women to be help meets.

Chapter 9 ~ Finding Your Life in His

I wonder if Yolanda's husband will quit his "dream come true" because she drops frequent reminders that nineteen years ago he didn't tell her that someday he was going to be a dairy farmer. Will her unhappy, over-worked expressions break his joy and rob him of his vision? If he does go back to being a full-time CPA, I wonder if he will spend the rest of his life dreaming of a different kind of lady for a wife, a bunch of happy children, and a barn full of milk cows? **Life is now.** Don't make him ruin his life by being forced to count someone else's money. Find your life in his.

God made us women to be **help meets,** and it is in our physical nature to be so. It is our spiritual calling and **God's perfect will for us.** It is the role in which we will succeed in life, and it is where we will find our very greatest fulfillment as a woman and as a saint of God. God said in Genesis, **"I will make him an help meet for him."** Paul said, **"For the man is not of the woman; but the woman of the man. Neither was the man created for the woman; but the woman for the man"** (I Corinthians 11:8-9). **"Unto the woman he said…and thy desire shall be to thy husband, and he shall rule over thee"** (Genesis 3:16).

> God is not looking for happy women to make them into help meets for men. He is looking for women willing to be true help meets, so he can fill them full of joy.

When we fight God's will and our husband's dreams, we are frustrated and disappointed. If our husbands are kind, *Steady Men*, like Yolanda's husband, they will eventually become discouraged and give up trying to please us. If our husbands are *Command Men*, they may leave us behind and find a dairy-loving woman. If our husbands are *Visionaries*, they will yell and make our life miserable until we run back to mama and end up sleeping in a cold bed and living on food stamps.

Life is full of choices. How you choose to respond will help decide your fate in life. **Life is now.** Learn to really enjoy taking out the trash or milking a cow. You will be amazed at how God will fill you full of himself. You will look back in your "happy" old age and rejoice at your lot in life and wonder how you could have ever been a long-faced sad sack. Someday people will say to you, "Your personality is just a happy type, and that is why you enjoy life. Isn't that right?" You can laugh

Life is full of choices ♥

128

and know that being in God's will is the only thing that makes you full of joy. God is not looking for happy women to make them into help meets for good men. He is looking for women willing to be true help meets to the men whom they married, so He can *fill* them full of joy.

His Express Image

We have studied three different types of men and how each one relates to the lady in his life. We have learned that God gives wisdom to those who ask. By now you know that it will take supernatural wisdom for you to come to know, accept, and appreciate your man as God made him. He may be all three different expressions at different times in his life, or he may be some of one and a lot of another. The important thing is for you to understand that he is what God made him, and that you are to be his suitable helper. Knowing what "expression" God has made him to be will help you become a better helper to the man of your life. God says so clearly and emphatically that, **"If any of you lack wisdom, let him ask of God, that giveth to all men** [and women] **liberally, and upbraideth not; and it shall be given him"** (James 1:5). Ask God to help you know and appreciate your man. Pray that God will give you the wisdom and grace to share your man's dreams so it will always be you that he dreams about.

TIME TO CONSIDER

Wisdom is knowing what you "bought" when you married that man <u>and</u> learning to adapt to him as he is, while enjoying the full value of your "purchase."

"Unto the woman he said...and thy desire shall be to thy husband, and he shall rule over thee" (Genesis 3:16).

➤ *Make a new habit.*

Is it God's will for your husband to adapt to you, or is it God's will for you to adapt to him? What habits in your life should you change to adapt to your husband's needs? Start today.

➤ *Getting Serious With God*

The word *WISDOM* appears 223 times in God's Word. As you look up and read each time the word *wisdom* appears, God will do a work in you and give you wisdom as you seek it. The Bible teaches that the sister of **wisdom** is God's commandments, and the kinswoman to **wisdom** is understanding (Prov. 7:4). Add to your diary your favorite **wisdom** verses. Establish one time each day that you will be reminded to ask God for wisdom. For instance, I have resolved for myself that when I stop at a red light, I will remember to pray for my husband. At every meal, we pray for both safety and **wisdom** for ourselves and our children. Write down a certain hour or occasion that will remind you to silently ask God for **wisdom** for yourself and for your husband.

Here are a few of my favorite wisdom verses:

"So teach us to number our days, that we may apply our hearts unto wisdom" (Psalm 90:12).
"To receive the instruction of wisdom, justice, and judgment, and equity" (Proverbs 1:3).
"So that thou incline thine ear unto wisdom, and apply thine heart to understanding" (Proverbs 2:2).
"Wisdom is the principal thing; therefore get wisdom: and with all thy getting get understanding" (Proverbs 4:7).

The
Jezebel Profile

Originally published in the No Greater Joy Magazine, June 2002
By Debi Pearl

Every day I read many letters from women who are having trouble in their marriage. I also receive letters from women testifying of the victory they have received and of healing that has occurred. I have developed a lot of insight through reading these testimonies of success and failure. My husband and I have searched the Scriptures to find answers for the many domestic issues that are presented to us.

The roots of marital failure are many and varied. There is no one cause or single issue. The man is at fault just as much as the woman, but it is nearly always the woman who seeks answers. Men just go to work and learn to live with it—or flee from it. Women ask, "What can I do to heal my marriage?" I am a woman. Men don't usually ask me for advice—which is as it should be. So I speak to women, and for that I am often accused of being one-sided. Women ask, "Why do you always blame the us? What about the men?" So to the women I say, you cannot change 100% of the marriage, but you can change 50% of it and that may improve your marriage by 200%.

Our readers are a unique group. They are spiritually minded, church going, Bible believing, mostly homeschooling, and very family centered in perspective. This profile lends itself to several unique sources of irritation to the marriage. Your letters and testimonies have enabled us to identify one of the most common problems on the woman's side: it is the Jezebel spirit.

When the name *Jezebel* comes to mind, most of us see the

painted face of a seductively dressed woman gazing into the eyes of a man who lacks good sense. But the Bible portrays Jezebel in a different light.

Revelation 2:20 says that Jezebel "calleth herself a prophetess," and men received her as a teacher. This was given as a warning to the church. The one whom you have received as a spirit-filled teacher comes to you in the great tradition of Jezebel. We have observed that many wives have stalled their half of the marriage by assuming the spiritual headship of the home. They would teach their husbands. But consider 1 Corinthians 14:34–35:

> **Let your women keep silence in the churches: for it is not permitted unto them to speak; but they are commanded to be under obedience, as also saith the law. And if they will learn any thing, let them ask their husbands at home: for it is a shame for women to speak in the church.**

I went back to 1 Kings to see what the Bible had to say about this woman Jezebel. The first thing I noticed was that Jezebel was more religious than her husband. She was spiritually intense. The Bible says in 1 Corinthians 11:3 "But I would have you know, that the head of every man is Christ; and the head of the woman is the man; and the head of Christ is God." As women, our place is under our husband, especially in the spiritual realm. Regardless of our circumstances, when we take the spiritual lead, we have stepped out from under our head. We have tried to rearrange God's designated place for us. We are no longer in God's will.

The second thing I observed was that Ahab was emotionally volatile—unstable. Is your husband prone to retreat? Is he bitter, angry, or depressed? When a woman takes the lead, she is playing the masculine role. Unless her husband fights her for supremacy, he must assume second place. And men who are forced into spiritual subjection to their wives tend to be angry and retreat like Ahab.

The third thing I noticed was that she used his emotional stress to endear herself to him—a strange way of lording over her husband. Jezebel manipulated and accused an innocent man, then had him murdered so that Ahab might have the vineyard he wanted. Ahab kept his face to the wall and let her do her dark deeds. Today if a woman is willing to play her husband's role in directing the family, he will lose his natural drive to bear responsibility.

In the dominant role, a woman quickly becomes emotionally and physically exhausted. God made us the weaker vessels. If you are in this exhausted state, then chances are you're carrying a load not meant for you. It is not for you to press your husband to do his duty to be spiritual. You are to live joyfully in the context he provides.

The fourth thing that jumped out at me was that Ahab could easily be manipulated by his wife to suit her purposes. Jezebel used him to set up images as aids to worship under her own prophets and to kill God's prophets. Often a man becomes involved in the church not because God has called him or because it is in his heart to do so, but because he is trying to please his wife and at least LOOK spiritual. When a husband steps into a spiritual role at his wife's beckoning, he becomes vulnerable to her guidance in that role. This is against nature and often brings conflict in the family and in the church.

Ahab chose not to notice when his wife worked behind the scenes. Many men turn their heads when they see their wives stepping out of their God-given role. These men would rather not have to deal with the stone-cold anger they would receive from their wives if they offered any resistance. Have you been there, done that?

Jezebel knew that she was not the rightful head, so she invoked her husband's name to give her word authority. Did you ever say, "Oh, my husband will not let me do that," when you knew in truth he really would not care? It is a way to maintain control and stop those who would question you. When a woman does this, she blocks any ministry God has to her.

Jezebel was deeply concerned about spiritual matters and took steps to help promote her spiritual leaders. In the process, she provoked her husband to destroy those in spiritual authority she did not like. Have you ever influenced your husband to think evil of those in authority because you did not like something about them? When a woman comes to this place, she might as well sign her name Jezebel.

God has a plan for women. He reveals his will in many verses in clear, concise commands. He gives a detailed picture of what he abhors in a woman by introducing us to Jezebel, then reaffirming in the New Testament just what it is about her character that he finds so despicable.

He reveals his will in the stories of women whom he honored. The story of Ruth tells of a young girl who knew tragedy, extreme poverty, and hard menial work, yet she maintained a positive, thankful, and submissive attitude. God blessed Ruth because her own personal success and happiness were not the driving forces in her life.

Esther is the story of a girl who lost all of her family and was taken by force to become the wife of an older, divorced, heathen man. She was put (by her husband's decree) in danger of losing her own life as well as the lives of all her people. Yet she overcame her circumstances and fear in order to honor her husband. The Scripture teaches that when her husband heard her honest appeal delivered with gracious dignity, she won his heart, and he turned to save her people. God used Esther because God's will was more important to her than her own fulfillment.

Proverbs 31 defines the virtuous woman. She is NOT a mousy, voiceless doormat. She is confident, hardworking, creative, and resourceful. She uses her time wisely and contributes to the family income. Her first virtue is that the heart of her husband is safe with her. It says that she will do him good and not evil all the days of her life. That is, he can trust her with his thoughts and feelings, never fearing that she might use the private knowledge she has of him to hurt him in any way. Some men maintain a distance from their wives because if they reveal themselves, their wives will use it against them when they are out of sorts.

If this passage had been written from our modern perspective, it would have extolled her for having a "quiet time," prayer time, and fellowship time, and would have projected an image of a prayer warrior, teacher, or counselor. In all the scriptural profiles of righteous women including Proverbs 31, none of those concepts are even mentioned. A Proverbs 31 woman is busy helping her husband become successful. She is too busy being productive to spend time being his conscience. In our culture, we have lost a clear understanding of what constitutes a virtuous woman. We have accepted the modern concept of the "spiritual" woman circulating in the realm of religious power and have forgotten that God does not see her in this same "glorious" light. What we think is spiritual, God labels Jezebel.

For my thoughts are not your thoughts, neither are your ways my ways, saith the LORD. Isaiah 55:8

In order to become a righteous woman, reaping the benefits of having our man adore us, we must follow God's principles of womanhood and totally reject the Jezebel tendency.

God laid down a few simple rules that must be followed because they are consistent with our feminine nature and the nature of men. It was Ruth's virtuous and humble, yet feminine, bold example that caused Boaz to love and admire her. It was Esther's submission to this principle that won the king's love and appreciation for her as a woman and as his queen. These women showed themselves womanly and lovable in the midst of extreme circumstances. God honored them with favor from the men in their lives.

Dominance and control are always masculine. It is a hormonal thing. It is the way God designed male nature. It is important for a woman to understand that she has to be feminine (devoid of dominance and control) in order for her man to view her as his exact counterpart and thus respond to her protectively, with love and gentleness.

God designed us, so he knows what a husband needs in order to function properly in his role as a man who cherishes the woman in his life. By nature, men need honor (this includes not questioning their decisions). They need respect (to be treated as if they are wise). They need reverence (to be daily admired as a man who is accomplishing great things). They need to be accepted for who and what they are, just like they are. Men need to feel they are in command and doing a good job.

An important part of man is a God-given, natural instinct to bring his wife pleasure. If a woman is to be greatly treasured, she will choose to find pleasure in the way the man presents himself and his care for her. All these traits are basic masculine needs. We were created as a helpmeet to the man we married, fulfilling who and what he is. This is God's will for us as women. When we obey God by responding to the needs of our husband, we are worshipping and honoring God.

Neither was the man created for the woman; but the woman for the man. 1 Corinthians 11:9

God created you to fulfill your husband's basic masculine needs. Only in that role will you find peace and cause your man to respond to you in loving adoration. This role of submission is totally feminine. It is the exact counterpart for his male needs.

And the LORD God said, It is not good that the man should be alone; I will make him an help meet for him. Genesis 2:18

A woman who criticizes her husband for watching too much TV no longer honors him. When a woman tries to control areas of their life together because she thinks she is right, she is usurping authority over him. A depressed, discontented woman who feels that her husband does not meet her needs is dishonoring God.

Hurt feelings are an attempt to control. Silence and emotional retreat are ugly, destructive ways to control both your husband and your children. Anger, sickness, exhaustion, and even fear are all used to control those you care about. Some women control their husband by having an intense spiritual hunger. Jezebel comes in many disguises.

There are many subtle ways to control and direct your husband. One of them is to tell your husband that you want him to be the spiritual leader in the home and then let him know that you are waiting to follow. You can lead from behind just by clearing your throat at the right moment. Many sweet homeschooling moms are the spiritual leaders in their homes. They play the masculine role spiritually. How this must grieve the Holy Spirit of God! Often the excuse is that we cannot serve two masters, and since our husband is carnal, we have to take the higher ground. Like Eve we are so deceived.

And Adam was not deceived, but the woman being deceived was in the transgression. 1 Timothy 2:14

A man cannot cherish a strong woman who has expressed her displeasure with him and is holding out until he fulfills her ideal. You say he should have Christ's love. Is that what you want? Do you want your husband to have to seek supernatural power just to find a way to love you? What most men cherish in their wives is the memory of when love was fun and free with no demands—the time when she smiled at him with a sweet, girlish, "I think you are wonderful" look. She was so feminine then, so much a woman. It was a time when he wanted to hold her just because she was his, a time when he wanted to give her everything. A vague memory keeps him hoping. He is as disappointed in love as you are—maybe more. He is just as lonely. He fills up his loneliness doing things that will distract him from the reality of the emptiness he knows is there but does not know how to fix. His helpmeet is not pleased with him. He is a loser.

The very first command God gave to a woman was

Thy desire shall be unto thy husband, and he shall rule over thee. Genesis 3:16

Is your desire toward your husband? Do you desire him as a man? Do you live to please him? Does he rule over you? This is God's will.

Being a Jezebel is an active role—actively controlling, actively doing our own thing. But being a Ruth or an Esther is just as active. It is a decision we make hundreds of times each day as we choose to joyfully honor our husband.

God's reward is without measure. Men are like clay in the hands of a woman whom they can trust with their hearts. A man, lost or saved, responds to a woman who honors him. When a woman looks to her husband with a face that is full of laughter and delight, he will look forward to being with her. If her voice speaks words of thanksgiving and joyful appreciation of him, he will want to listen to her. If her actions are full of service and creativity, and if she has goodwill toward him, he will be drawn to her as a bee is to honey. This kind of lady is altogether feminine. She is what God created and gave to Adam.

Deep in our heart we all want the same thing. We all want to be loved and cherished. We all cry out with our utmost being to be treasured in the heart of our husband. It is the greatest honor on earth to know your husband is thrilled that you are his woman. It passes all of earth's blessings to feel his gaze upon you and know that you are his greatest gift, his most prized possession, his best friend, his favorite pastime, his only chum, and his delight as a lover. It is a great joy to know that he is proud you are his. It is not remembering birthdays, opening the door of a car, or other silly customs that we crave; it is the knowledge that he is totally taken with us. We want him to want us. We simply want to be loved. It is God's perfect will for our husbands to love us. It is God's perfect will for us to honor, obey, and reverence our husbands. God's way works. If what you are doing this year has not worked, why not go God's way?

> **For a man indeed ought not to cover his head, forasmuch as he is the image and glory of God: but the woman is the glory of the man.**
>
> **For the man is not of the woman; but the woman of the man.**
>
> **Neither was the man created for the woman; but the woman for the man. 1 Corinthians 11:7–9**

Created to Be His Help Meet
10th Anniversary Edition

What God is doing through this book is amazing! We've received thousands of letters from wives and husbands giving testimony to marriages restored and old loves rekindled. Regardless of how you began your marriage or how dark and lonely the path that has brought you to where you are now, I want you to know that it is possible today to have a marriage so good and so fulfilling that it can only be explained as a miracle.

Amazon Best-Seller
& Amazon Top 100
out of 22 million
books!

336-page book. Available in 12 languages.
Contact us for more information.

Single volumes or case quantity of 24 (40% discount). MP3 audio CD also available (English only).

The Help Meet's Journey

The Journey is a 184-page year-long companion journal for *Created to Be His Help Meet*. There are extra pages for your stories, doodlings, studies, and pictures where you will create a lasting memory of the miracle God is doing in you. This is a perfect study guide for individuals or women's study groups. Available in single volumes or case quantity of 24 (40% discount). *184-page workbook journal.*

Preparing to Be a Help Meet

Being a good help meet starts long before marriage. It is a mindset, a learned habit, a way of life established as a young unmarried girl—or at least that's the way it should be. This is a perfect study guide for individuals or women's study groups. ***Preparing to Be a Help Meet*** continues with the ever-popular concept of the three kinds of men introduced in ***Created to Be His Help Meet***. This follow-up work discusses the three kinds of girls and what type of man best suits each. Are you a Go-to Girl, or a Servant, or maybe a Dreamer? How can you get the attention of a good man who best suits you? Find out how to avoid being a Hidden Flower or a Grabber. Discover what you can be doing now that will help your future husband succeed in his life and business. Find all these answers and more in Debi's book. Available in English or Spanish. ***296-page book.***

Amazon Best-Seller & Amazon Top 100 out of 22 million books!

Single volumes or case quantity of 24 (40% discount).
MP3 audio CD also available (English only).

Created to NEED a Help Meet
A Marriage Guide for Men

Men know they need their wives sexually, but most don't know they need their wives emotionally, spiritually, and mentally in order to be well-rounded, thoughtful, balanced, and motivated men. Written for men, but in the very same personal style as *Created to Be His Help Meet*. Built on Scripture. One reader said that this book is a *"gritty, witty, no-holds-barred excursion into relationships and marital bliss!"* ***245-page book.***

Amazon Best-Seller out of 22 million books!

Single volumes or case quantity of 24 (40% discount). MP3 audio CD also available (read by Nathan Pearl, Mike and Debi's son).

In Search of a Help Meet

For men ages 18 and up. Choosing your wife is one of the most important and life directing decision you will ever make. This book may save you from making the biggest mistake of your life. In today's world, finding that perfect woman is a difficult art or maybe a far-out gamble, and few find the lady of their dreams. Making a good choice starts with knowledge of what you need, and how to spot the gal who has your number. Choosing the type of woman who not only turns you on but also relates well to you is the key to a glorious marriage. I guess the real issue is that most guys don't have a clue as to what makes women tick and they sure don't know what they should be looking for. This is a clear, focused plan for becoming a man of honor, getting primed for marriage and guidance in the search for the right lady.

Single volumes or case quantity of 24 (40% discount). MP3 audio CD also available (English only). *248-page book.*

The Bible on Divorce and Remarriage

Historically, Christians have been divided on the issue of divorce and remarriage, many institutions coming down on the side that it is adultery to remarry while one's former spouse is still alive. This is inconsistent with the words of Jesus in Matthew and the words of the Apostle Paul in Romans. Others stand by the words of Paul in Corinthians where he clearly declares that it is not a sin to marry again if you were "put away" (abandoned or divorced) by an unbelieving spouse. There seems to be a conflict in Scripture regarding divorce and remarriage. You do not have to pick a side to the exclusion of the other. There is marvelous harmony. In this book you will see Scripture like you've never seen before. *96-page book.*

Holy Sex

Michael Pearl takes his readers through a refreshing journey of Biblical texts, centered in the Song of Solomon. This sanctifying look at the most powerful passion God ever created will free the reader from false guilt and inhibition. Michael Pearl says, "It is time for Christian couples to take back this sacred ground and enjoy the holy gift of sexual pleasure." *82-page book.*

Marriage God's Way Video

A perfect marriage is 100/100. It is a man and a woman giving 100% to the other. What if he or she won't give 100%? Then you can match their 10% with your 10% and continue in an unfulfilling relationship, or, by the grace of God and the power of the Holy Spirit, you can give 100% to your spouse for their sake and watch their 10% grow into 100%. Michael takes the viewer through the Word of God to uncover the Divine plan for husbands and wives. *2 DVD set.*

To Betroth or Not to Betroth

All Christian parents want their children to have God's first and best in all areas of their lives, and this includes marriage. In an effort to avoid the dangers of the modern dating game, families are giving attention to the concept of betrothal. The dangers of the betrothal system are exposed with biblical truth, bringing objectivity back to an often-misunderstood subject. By Michael Pearl. 28 pages.

Young Adults & Marriage

The first crop of homeschoolers are either married or ready for marriage. This message, taught by Michael Pearl in California, was given to help parents and their young adult children make wise decisions. It has the story of all five of his children finding their mates. It should prove entertaining. By Michael Pearl. Audio CD, 54 min.

Good & Evil Graphic Novel

Award winning, illustrated novel, 330 pages of dazzling full color art work telling the Bible story chronologically from Genesis to Revelation. Written by Michael Pearl and drawn by Danny Bulanadi, a retired Marvel Comic Book artist. Now in 45 languages, popular with missionaries and youth workers, this book has tremendous appeal to all ages and cultures—great as Sunday School curriculum. *330-page book.*

FREE Email and Magazine Subscriptions

Hug Often

FREE weekly emails with specials, articles, large discounts or **FREE SHIPPING** (sometimes both), **PLUS** our bi-monthly digital magazine and much more! The **FREE** bi-monthly No Greater Joy print magazine is full of articles on family relations, child training, and more.

Subscribe today at www.nogreaterjoy.org/free-subscription

NGJ is a 501(c)3 Non-profit Organization dedicated to serving families with the good news of Jesus Christ.